DATA ANALYTICS IN FOOTBALL

Data Analytics in Football provides students, researchers and coaches with a firm grounding in the principles of modern performance analysis. It offers an insight into the use of positional data, exploring how they can be collected, modelled, analysed and interpreted. Introducing cutting-edge methods, the book challenges long-held assumptions and encourages a new way of thinking about football analysis.

Based on data collected from the German Bundesliga and the UEFA Champions League, the book seeks to define the role of positional data in football match analysis by exploring topics such as:

- What is positional data analysis and how did it emerge from conventional match analysis?
- How can positional data be collected and which technologies can be used?
- What are the benefits of a data-driven approach to decision making in football?
- What Key Performance Indicators based on positional data should be used?
- How can traditional match analysis be complemented by using positional data and advanced KPIs?
- How can these new methods evolve in the future?

Accessibly written, packed full of examples from elite football and supplemented with expert interviews (Ralf Rangnick, Urs Siegenthaler and others), *Data Analytics in Football* is a thought-provoking, rigorously evidence-based guide to the use of data analytics in football performance analysis. As such, it is a vital resource for any student, researcher or coach interested in performance analysis and skill acquisition, or anyone interested in football more generally.

Daniel Memmert is Professor and Executive Head of the Institute of Training and Computer Science in Sport at the German Sport University Cologne, Germany.

Dominik Raabe is Research Assistant at the Institute of Training and Computer Science in Sport at the German Sport University Cologne, Germany. He is also studying Scientific Computing (MSc) at the Institute of Mathematics at the Technical University Berlin.

DATA ANALYTICS IN FOOTBALL

Positional Data Collection, Modelling and Analysis

Daniel Memmert and Dominik Raabe

Routledge
Taylor & Francis Group

LONDON AND NEW YORK

First published in English 2018
by Routledge
2 Park Square, Milton Park, Abingdon, Oxon OX14 4RN

and by Routledge
711 Third Avenue, New York, NY 10017

Routledge is an imprint of the Taylor & Francis Group, an informa business

© 2018 Daniel Memmert and Dominik Raabe

The right of Daniel Memmert and Dominik Raabe to be identified as authors
of this work has been asserted by them in accordance with sections 77 and 78
of the Copyright, Designs and Patents Act 1988.

British Library Cataloguing-in-Publication Data
A catalogue record for this book is available from the British Library

Library of Congress Cataloging-in-Publication Data
Names: Memmert, Daniel, author. | Raabe, Dominik, author.
Title: Data analytics in football : positional data collection, modelling and
analysis / Daniel Memmert and Dominik Raabe.
Description: Abingdon, Oxon ; New York, NY : Routledge, 2018. |
Includes bibliographical references and index.
Identifiers: LCCN 2017058008 (print) | LCCN 2018012668 (ebook) |
ISBN 9781351210164 (Master eBk) | ISBN 9781351210157 (Web PDF) |
ISBN 9781351210157 (ePub3) | ISBN 9781351210133 (Mobipocket/
Kindle) | ISBN 9780815381549 (hbk) | ISBN 9780815381556 (pbk) |
ISBN 9781351210164 (ebk)
Subjects: LCSH: Soccer—Data processing. | Soccer—Statistical methods. |
Soccer—Mathematical models. | Quantitative research.
Classification: LCC GV943 (ebook) | LCC GV943 .M385 2018 (print) |
DDC 796.33—dc23
LC record available at https://lccn.loc.gov/2017058008

Translation from the German language edition:
Revolution im Profifußball Mit Big Data zur Spielanalyse 4.0
by Daniel Memmert and Dominik Raabe
Copyright © Springer-Verlag GmbH Deutschland 2017
This Springer imprint is published by Springer Nature
The registered company is Springer-Verlag GmbH

ISBN: 978-0-8153-8154-9 (hbk)
ISBN: 978-0-8153-8155-6 (pbk)
ISBN: 978-1-351-21016-4 (ebk)

Typeset in Bembo and Stone Sans
by Florence Production Ltd, Stoodleigh, Devon, UK

CONTENTS

Preface by Hansi Flick   *vii*
Preface by Ralf Rangnick   *ix*
Acknowledgements   *xi*

1   Where is the revolution?   1

2   A historical perspective on positional data   13

3   Technological background   35

4   Collecting data in the Bundesliga   43

5   In search of the Holy Grail   49

6   Betting and sports analytics   65

7   Where are they running?   71

8   From media to storytelling   77

9   Key properties of long-term success in football   85

10   The key to success   93

11   Reasons for dominance   99

12 FCB versus FCB   105

13 The myth of home advantage   123

14 Managerial influence   127

15 All on attack   133

16 Laws of a derby   137

17 Who will be nominated for the FIFA World Cup 2018?   147

18 Conclusion   153

Index   *173*

PREFACE

Hansi Flick

Across all levels and age groups there are a variety of factors that are responsible for long-term fun and success for football teams. Among of these factors are technique, physical condition and cognition. In recent years especially, tactical aspects have gained importance. The value of match plans increases—and they have to cover more and more possible scenarios. As a consequence, coaches and assistant coaches have to invest more work into the preparation to observe and evaluate all aspects of the game. And this takes time, a lot of time.

Therefore a specific field of profession has developed: game analytics. This offers a wide range of options in diagnosis and training control for the coaching staff, not least because of the technical developments in this field. However, "traditional" video analyses are time consuming even for these specialists, in particular because complex game situations have to be determined and decoded manually.

This book gives an overview of the genesis of the "game analysis." In addition to this, it shows that information about the complexity of the game can be generated automatically and in seconds with the help of a new methodological approach. Its basis is data that we have been collecting from Die Mannschaft (German Men's Football National Team) for more than ten years at the German Football Association (Deutscher Fußball Bund, DFB): positional data! Now these can be ennobled thanks to new technical developments.

In practice the value of positional data is mainly in regard to the control of work load and physical stress. The integration of positional data in tactical analyses has been not yet been utilized—although it would be possible to use these. At this point, sport science and sports computer science, as well as the analysts, are equally in high demand. Their task is to translate these data into a practical context: the challenge is to not only use the technical possibilities to generate Big Data, but also to purposively manage the development of players and teams.

In the sportive mission statement of the DFB we rooted the game vision as our fundament. Besides the individual game concept that each coach can shape according to his or her team's abilities, we have defined independent guidelines in our concept of the game and put these at the forefront of the conception. These form a kind of "quality characteristic" for the understanding of the game. According to the idea of the game (to score goals) it is, for example, indispensable for us to recognize and use spaces behind opponents when attacking. This applies to anyone who plays football, no matter where and at what age.

It is important to be able to assess the skills based on the guidelines quickly, reliably and objectively. And this requires the inclusion of positional data beyond the video-based approach. Ultimately, we are talking about geometry and physics, in other words cofigurations, directions, angles and speeds. All of this makes up positional data. When we take advantage of this potential, we can completely redefine and maybe even revolutionize in particular the spotting of talent.

Dear football fans, I hope you have a good time and gain new knowledge through reading this great book.

Yours,
Hansi Flick
Former Sports director of the German Football Association

PREFACE

Ralf Rangnick

Today, modern match analysis must offer more than the bare evaluation of tackle rates and distances covered, as it has become obvious that these are not, *per se*, the difference between victory and defeat. Rather, it is a significantly more complex analysis with more performance indicators that is going to provide new insights into elite football. Big Data—or the so called "positional data"—help in recognizing tactical patterns, as nowadays these are able to track the position of each player and the ball very accurately. As a consequence, I have always put emphasis on the importance of a competent and well-equipped analysis department for modern match analysis, at all my previous coaching jobs as well as in my current profession as sports director. So I constantly tried rapidly to adapt to new methodological and digital trends to use these for our games during my time with VfB Stuttgart, Hannover 96, 1899 Hoffenheim, Schalke 04 and recently in Leipzig.

The Institute of Training and Computer Science in Sport has been one of the leading institutions in the development and testing of advanced key performance indicators based on positional data. Therefore it is only consequent and logical that the first book about Big Data in elite sports is presented by these authors. To apply this knowledge systematically to our regular training and practices is going to be the next step.

Dear readers, I wish you much pleasure in reading this book, and success and joy with the world's greatest pastime.

Yours,
Ralf Rangnick
Sports Director, RB Leipzig

ACKNOWLEDGEMENTS

At this point, we would like to thank our experts for their knowledge:

Ralf Rangnick (Sports Director, RB Leipzig)
Urs Siegenthaler (Head Scout, German National Team)
Prof. Martin Lames (TU Munich)
Lars O.D. Christensen (Talent Development and Training, FC Midtjylland)
Prof. Jürgen Perl (University of Mainz)
Tim Bagner (ChyronHego, Account Manager Deutsche Fußball-Liga (German Football League))
Hansi Flick (Former Sports Director of the German Football Association)
Ulrich Forstner (National Coach 'Science and Education', German Hockey Association)
Dr Holger Broich (Head of Health and Fitness of Bayern Munich)
Ernst Tanner (Head of Youth Department, FC Red Bull Salzburg)
Dr Hendrik Weber (Head of Technology and Innovation, Deutsche Fußball-Liga (German Football League))
Dr Daniel Link (TU Munich)
Prof. Arnold Baca (University of Vienna)
Dominik Meffert (German Sports University Cologne)
Prof. Dr Matthias Lochmann (University of Erlangen)
Chuck Korb (Senior Analyst, Boston Bruins)
Stefan Wagner (Global General Manager Sports & Entertainment, SAP SE)
Joachim Holzmüller (FIFA, Head of Football Technology Innovation)

1

WHERE IS THE REVOLUTION?

Big Data in professional sports

"We want a revolution," says Christofer Clemens, head analyst of the Germany national football team in an interview with the football magazine *11Freunde*. And he carries on: "We want to completely scrutinize match analysis." The heart of this revolution is constituted by the huge amount of data which high performance football has been diligently accumulating for years now. Big Data has football under control, just like in many other areas of our daily lives. It is about time to draw the right conclusions from this treasure of information. Already by 2015, the Institute of Training and Computer Science in Sport at the German Sport University in Cologne had started the first post-professional Master's degree, M.A. Game Analysis. Central aims: nurturing innovation and creativity in working with game data.

It is only possible to innovatively work in practice and understand constant changes as continuity with scientific know-how. The requirements of game analysis as a professional field have risen since athletic demands have evolved, due to increasing professionalization in sports games. Therefore, it involves finding new paths for the analysis and interpretation of video and positional data.

In the future, match analysts will be involved more frequently in the athletic performance of their teams. They will be involved in the development of game ideas and the generation of solutions for specific problems in particular. The demand of game analysis data is further growing with intensive usage in broadcasting. Media professionals will have to be able to comprehend data in the context of the game and understandably communicate these. Last, but not least, it takes highly qualified specialists to develop analysis methods for evaluation, analysis and presentation of analysis data on an advanced level.

As Ralf Rangnick mentioned in his Foreword, match analysis nowadays includes more than the counting of tackles, received passes, or distance completed. These conventional parameters, collectively called *event-data*, provide quite concrete insights into the world's favorite sport. However, scientific studies demonstrate that they hardly deliver any clues regarding the final outcome of a game. Yet, guided by the large-scale introduction of positional data in professional football during the last years, a completely new perspective has opened up which only waits to be utilized.

The German Hockey federation, which has been promoting innovative game analysis for several years, has also recognized this:

> Take Bayern Munich in football: Recently, their opponents had it very comfortable with Bayern's constant passing game in which personal elements did not play a role anymore. Every now and then we have also experienced it like this: We constantly work but remain completely ineffective. The aim has to be to unsettle the opponent much more frequently. At the end not even the opponent analysts that evaluate everything and present it in 50 page glossy brochures to their teams should know what will happen with the Germans.
>
> Valentin Altenburg, August 7, 2016, 4:45 p.m.;
> source: *ZeitOnline*

This statement on the game analysis of tomorrow was given by the Germany national hockey team coach Valentin Altenburg, just before the XXXIst Olympic Games, 2016, in Brazil. Afterwards he won the bronze medal with his team. He indirectly encouraged the fact that we need new impulses and innovations despite the knowledge of quantitative and qualitative game analysis. How reliable are our key performance indicators (KPIs)? Which interpretation is possible? What does it mean for the training schedule?

One possibility of realization can be found within the term Big Data. Positional data have been providing a new standard for a couple of years now, in order to view teams' variability and flexibility in a better way and extract constant patterns more precisely. Advanced techniques nowadays enable us to detect the location of every player on the field. Thereby, every action of the players on the field can be registered manually or with the use of (semi)-automated methods.

In practice, various technical procedures show the position of all players in the form of X–Y-coordinates—and at best in real time. The captured data are described as *positional* or *tracking data*. Either special camera systems or mobile devices, which the players wear under their shirts, are used for data collection. The subsequent analysis based on these positional data can be generated in just a few seconds. Whenever a team accomplishes a successful move, it is divided into its component parts in the blink of an eye—including tactical details of offensive as well as defensive behavior of their own and the opposing team.

Predominantly based on video data, the modern standard is that analysts and coaches use the information gathered on physical, technical, and tactical player and team performance to optimize training processes or for game preparation.

However, objective performance acquisition using digital data is still not living up to its full potential. The experiences of recent years have clearly shown that the capability of theories and methods based on sport sciences, especially in the area of positional data, does not yet cover the needs of high-performance sport.

Current research focuses on how robust findings in football and other team and racket sports can be generated by means of modern procedures using computer science and statistics. The heart of this is the highly complex, but for practical issues indispensable, question of how the tactical and technical components of a match can be analyzed in such a way that relevant conclusions for coaching decisions can be made. Only in this way is it possible to optimally utilize the ever-growing flood of data to increase competitiveness (Memmert et al., 2016a; Memmert & Rein, 2018).

To get one step closer to this goal, sport scientists are constantly developing and testing elaborate KPIs, which are supposed to deliver information on player performance. Even though promising approaches can be detected within these, there is still a visible deficit in the practical establishment of such performance parameters. To date, only a small number of procedures and methods have brought it close to marketability, as empirical testing is behind schedule. There is an obvious lack of field studies in the professional realm that would complement theory with practical insights (Memmert et al., 2016b).

FIGURE 1.1 FIFA World Cup Final 2006: Italy 6, France 4 (a.e.t.). To our knowledge, this is one of the first games in which positional data were measured (a. Zinedine Zidane (FRA) and Gennaro Gattuso (ITA); b. positional data; c. graphic map of positional data)

Source: Eddy Lemaistre/Corbis Sport/Getty Images

continued . . .

```
Ball        ;Buffon   ;Grosso   ;Materazzi  ;Cannavaro ;Zambrotta ;Camoranesi;Perrota  ;Pirlo   ;De Rossi              ;Gattuso
                                                                              :To

52.04,33.13,0.00;10.00,36.00;34.00,22.97;28.97,30.00;28.20,39.00;29.97,50.00;50.97,60.88;51.00,12.00;40.00,31.00;-65000.00,-65000.00;40.00,36.02;51
52.04,33.13,0.00;10.00,36.00;34.00,22.97;28.97,30.00;28.25,39.00;29.97,50.00;50.97,60.93;51.00,12.00;40.00,31.00;-65000.00,-65000.00;40.00,36.02;51
52.04,33.13,0.00;10.00,36.00;34.00,22.97;28.97,30.00;28.27,39.00;29.97,50.00;50.97,60.93;51.00,12.00;40.00,31.00;-65000.00,-65000.00;40.00,36.02;51
52.04,33.13,0.00;10.00,36.00;34.00,22.96;28.97,30.00;28.30,39.00;29.97,50.00;50.97,60.94;51.00,12.00;40.00,31.00;-65000.00,-65000.00;40.00,36.04;51
52.04,33.13,0.00;10.00,36.00;34.00,22.96;28.97,30.00;28.34,39.00;29.97,50.00;50.97,60.96;51.00,12.00;40.00,31.00;-65000.00,-65000.00;40.00,36.04;51
52.04,33.13,0.00;10.00,36.00;34.00,22.95;28.97,30.00;28.38,39.00;29.97,50.00;50.97,61.00;51.02,12.00;40.00,31.00;-65000.00,-65000.00;40.00,36.05;51
52.04,33.13,0.00;10.00,36.00;34.00,22.95;28.97,30.00;28.43,39.00;29.97,50.00;50.97,61.02;51.02,12.00;40.00,31.00;-65000.00,-65000.00;40.00,36.06;51
52.04,33.13,0.00;10.00,36.00;34.00,22.94;28.97,30.00;28.46,39.00;29.97,50.00;50.97,61.02;51.02,12.00;40.00,31.00;-65000.00,-65000.00;40.00,36.09;51
52.04,33.13,0.00;10.00,36.00;34.00,22.93;28.97,30.00;28.51,39.00;29.97,50.00;50.97,61.03;51.03,12.00;40.00,30.97;-65000.00,-65000.00;40.00,36.11;51
52.04,33.13,0.00;10.00,36.00;34.00,22.93;28.97,30.00;28.54,39.00;29.97,50.00;50.97,61.05;51.05,12.00;40.00,30.97;-65000.00,-65000.00;40.00,36.13;51
52.03,33.25,0.00;10.00,36.00;34.00,22.92;28.97,30.00;28.59,39.00;29.97,50.00;50.97,61.06;51.06,12.00;40.00,30.97;-65000.00,-65000.00;40.00,36.14;51
52.02,33.48,0.05;10.00,36.00;34.00,22.89;28.97,30.00;28.62,39.00;29.97,50.00;50.97,61.09;51.09,12.00;40.00,30.97;-65000.00,-65000.00;40.00,36.18;51
52.02,33.52,0.09;10.00,36.00;34.00,22.87;28.97,30.00;28.67,39.00;29.97,50.00;50.97,61.10;51.10,12.00;40.00,30.96;-65000.00,-65000.00;40.00,36.20;51
52.02,33.65,0.12;10.00,36.00;34.00,22.85;28.97,30.00;28.69,38.97;29.97,50.00;50.97,61.12;51.11,12.00;40.00,30.96;-65000.00,-65000.00;40.00,36.25;51
52.00,33.79,0.14;10.00,36.00;34.00,22.85;28.97,30.00;28.72,38.97;29.97,50.00;50.97,61.12;51.12,12.00;40.00,30.96;-65000.00,-65000.00;40.00,36.29;51
52.00,33.91,0.15;10.00,36.00;34.00,22.81;28.97,30.00;28.76,38.97;29.97,50.02;50.97,61.10;51.14,12.00;40.00,30.95;-65000.00,-65000.00;40.00,36.30;51
52.00,34.04,0.15;10.00,36.00;34.00,22.78;28.97,30.00;28.78,38.97;29.97,50.02;50.97,61.18;51.18,12.01;40.00,30.95;-65000.00,-65000.00;40.00,36.36;51
51.98,34.18,0.14;10.00,36.00;34.00,22.76;28.97,30.00;28.81,38.96;29.97,50.02;50.97,61.25;51.20,12.02;40.00,30.94;-65000.00,-65000.00;40.00,36.36;51
51.98,34.31,0.12;10.00,36.00;34.00,22.72;28.97,30.00;28.84,38.96;29.97,50.02;50.97,61.27;51.25,12.05;40.00,30.93;-65000.00,-65000.00;40.00,36.38;51
51.98,34.45,0.09;10.00,36.00;34.00,22.68;28.97,30.00;28.86,38.95;29.97,50.03;50.97,61.30;51.27,12.05;40.00,30.92;-65000.00,-65000.00;40.00,36.43;51
51.96,34.57,0.05;10.00,36.00;34.00,22.67;28.97,30.00;28.88,38.95;29.97,50.05;50.97,61.34;51.30,12.06;40.00,30.92;-65000.00,-65000.00;40.00,36.46;51
51.97,34.66,0.00;10.00,36.00;34.00,22.61;28.97,30.00;28.89,38.95;29.97,50.06;50.97,61.38;51.36,12.09;40.00,30.89;-65000.00,-65000.00;40.00,36.52;51
51.97,34.57,0.00;10.00,36.00;34.00,22.59;28.97,30.00;28.93,38.95;29.97,50.06;50.97,61.43;51.39,12.10;40.00,30.87;-65000.00,-65000.00;40.00,36.54;51
51.97,34.61,0.00;10.00,36.00;34.00,22.53;28.97,30.00;28.93,38.93;29.97,50.11;50.97,61.46;51.43,12.13;40.00,30.85;-65000.00,-65000.00;40.00,36.59;51
51.97,34.57,0.00;10.00,36.00;34.00,22.51;28.97,30.00;28.93,38.90;29.97,50.12;50.97,61.52;51.47,12.14;40.00,30.84;-65000.00,-65000.00;40.00,36.63;51
51.97,34.54,0.00;10.00,36.00;33.97,22.45;28.97,30.00;28.94,38.89;29.97,50.15;50.97,61.52;51.52,12.17;40.00,30.81;-65000.00,-65000.00;40.00,36.65;51
51.97,34.52,0.00;10.00,36.00;33.97,22.43;28.97,30.00;28.95,38.87;29.97,50.15;50.97,61.59;51.59,12.21;40.00,30.78;-65000.00,-65000.00;40.00,36.70;51
51.97,34.52,0.00;10.00,36.00;33.97,22.36;28.97,30.00;28.96,38.86;29.97,50.21;50.97,61.62;51.61,12.25;40.00,30.76;-65000.00,-65000.00;40.00,36.72;51
51.97,34.45,0.00;10.00,36.00;33.97,22.36;28.97,30.00;28.96,38.86;29.97,50.21;50.97,61.65;51.65,12.27;40.00,30.72;-65000.00,-65000.00;40.00,36.77;51
51.97,34.42,0.00;10.00,36.00;33.97,22.34;28.97,30.00;28.96,38.84;29.97,50.25;50.97,61.69;51.71,12.30;40.00,30.68;-65000.00,-65000.00;40.02,36.79;51
```

FIGURE 1.1 Continued

Source: Eddy Lemaistre/Corbis Sport/Getty Images

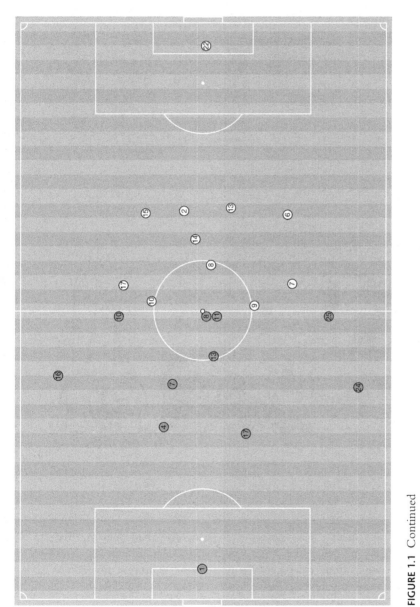

FIGURE 1.1 Continued

Source: Eddy Lemaistre/Corbis Sport/Getty Images

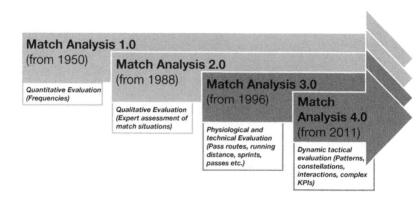

FIGURE 1.2 From game analysis 1.0 to game analysis 4.0

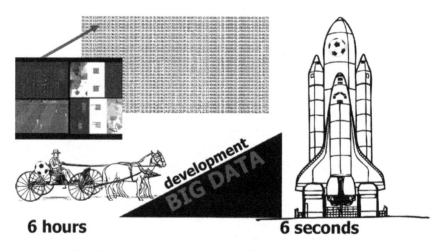

FIGURE 1.3 The digital revolution in elite football: game analysis provided in a matter of seconds thanks to Big Data

The fundamentals have nevertheless been established, and the data era has already grabbed football in its claws. On the following pages we will describe some exciting results, from which game analysis 1.0–4.0 and in the future even 5.0 can change and develop football (see Table 1.1). At first we will follow the development of game analysis in general and match analysis based on positional data, in particular from its infancy to the status quo. Subsequently, we take a look behind the curtain regarding the techniques used, data material, situation in both the Bundesliga and European football, as well as an outlook on the everyday life of game analysts in other types of sport.

On this journey, we will not forget to look frequently at how technological progress can further impact football as we know it. The catalyst of the proliferated usage of data is the fact that analyses with positional data can be run completely automatically and can deliver insights into the game online. Numerous expert interviews from both theory and practice also deliver new perspectives and how the data revolution is about to sustainably redefine modern sports.

The second major component of this book is the elaboration of findings that computer-based game analysis already provides us with today. The data used are based on a competitive project, tendered by the German Football League (DFL), with the title: Positional Data in High Performance Football. This project, which was carried out in 2015 by the Institute of Training and Computer Science in Sport of the German Sport University, is, to our knowledge one of the first large-scale field studies in the area of positional data analysis. A team of mathematicians, computer scientists, and match analysts worked on this project with the central aim of evaluating a selection of KPIs, newly developed automatically with the use of neuronal networks, and to test them over a whole season of Bundesliga football.

Nowadays we are able to extract distinctive tactical patterns from positional data (Grunz, Memmert, & Perl, 2012). To do so, specific neuronal networks that help to classify single predefined moves are used. In larger validation studies, for example, short and long game openings, throw-ins, corners, and free kicks were extracted from the positional data in fractions of seconds and connected with the respective video sequence. In this way the tactical pattern, which was read out by a computer, could be compared to the patterns which were found manually by a match analyst. As you can see from Table 1.1, congruities greater than 80 per cent can be recognized. Considering that if two or three match analysts and their results were compared to each other, there would also be congruity rates of this level, one can assume good accuracy.

TABLE 1.1 Congruity rates between human and machine regarding detection of tactical patterns in football matches (Grunz, Memert, & Perl, 2012)

Category	Number of cases of conventional match analysis	Congruity with net-based match analysis	Detection rate
Game openings	131	110	91 %
Throw-ins	27	27	100 %
Free kicks	16	14	92 %
Corners	12	12	100 %

The study consisted of 50 matches taken from the 2014–2015 season. The matches were analyzed and over 11,000 performance values were automatically generated and subsequently evaluated in terms of various exploratory hypotheses. The core of the analysis formed the in-house-developed analysis tool SOCCER (© Perl, 2011), which combines conventional data analysis, dynamic state-event-modeling, and artificial neuronal networks. The latter is the offspring of modern neurosciences and has also turned out to be highly beneficial in data analysis and machine learning.

The SOCCER package has been developed in the context of four projects, which were funded by the German Research Foundation (PE 445/7–1, ME 2678/3–1, ME 2678/3–2, ME 2678/3–3), and of two projects of the Federal Institute for Sport Science (VF 0407/06/12/2001–2002, VF 07/06/04/2005–2006), since 2001. The projects proceeded through cooperation between the Institute for Computer Science of the University of Mainz (Prof. Jürgen Perl) and the Institute of Sports and Sports Sciences of the Heidelberg University (Dr. Daniel Memmert), and have been continued at the German Sport University in Cologne (Dr. Daniel Memmert) since 2011 (see also the publications at www.dshs-koeln.de/en/institut-fuer-trainingswissenschaft-und-sportinformatik/).

On the basis of numerous examples from the Bundesliga and other leagues in European top-class sport, we want to give you a detailed insight on how different tactical aspects can be modeled, and how individual matches or even entire seasons can be analyzed by a single mouse-click and subsequently interpreted. The results should not only provide an exciting glance behind the scenes of professional football, but also question one's beliefs and convictions concerning football tactics at the highest level in sports and initiate new ways of thinking.

INTERVIEW WITH THE HEAD SCOUT OF THE GERMAN MEN'S NATIONAL FOOTBALL TEAM, URS SIEGENTHALER

In a similar vein to the men's hockey national coach Valentin Altenburg, the head scout of the Germany national football team, Urs Siegenthaler, likewise judges the situation of match analysis. With FC Basel, Siegenthaler won the national championship five times and the cup twice. He ended his career after seasons at Neuchâtel Xamax and Young Boys Bern at FC Basel. In 1978, he completed his coaching certificate at the German Sport University Cologne, and from 1987 to 1990 he was head coach of FC Basel then assistant coach of the Swiss National Team. Since 2005, Urs Siegenthaler has been chief scout for the German national team. In the following interview, he talks about a new vision that he connects to scouting and match analysis: ideas that can be approached on the basis of positional data in the near or remote future, or even solved and implemented.

Dear Mr. Siegenthaler, how exactly do you prepare for tournaments?

In the months before a big tournament, I always try to experience the development of different sports in order to get a different, possibly new picture on the development of sports. Development is an observation, linked to perception. This gets me motivated to check and question my own past theses and work.

How do you look upon your task as a scout?

How often did I ask myself in the past: What am I doing here? Put my foot in it with my interrogation "what do I mean by this is a good one?" Especially the last tournaments, UEFA EC, FIFA WC and the XXXIth Olympics should be a hint for us that the other nations are not sleeping!

How exactly can scouting be understood? In play, doesn't a lot happen just by chance or by something different?

What got my attention in the recent past? Is it just teams or players, who couldn't perform? Did the football god turn against these 'losers'? Or was there a change, a development in sports in general and especially in the sport of football after all? If the answer is yes, what and how did the sport, the players, the observation of a match, a perceived development change? Should we still link the match observation to the aspect that we watch and evaluate matches in a well-tried form?

So, should we understand something different by match observation?

Yes. My intuition tells me that the term is outdated and that match observation by itself is outworn. Wouldn't "trend observer" be a better expression and "further research" another, maybe even better, description for my work for the DFB?

Plenty of questions, but what exactly do we know about it currently?

The sport of football has changed at the level of the Top 100 and this to the disadvantage of the supposedly better ones! However, there was one simple, small change.

Why is this to the disadvantage of the supposedly better one?

The stronger one is forced to face defensive superiority! Everyone, teams and players, have leveled out at this general standard – good technique, good tactical guidelines, stamina and willingness to run, good coordinative skills and, ultimately, a good personal attitude and a commitment to the task respectively!

And referring to the training: Are the changes here as well just very moderate?

Yes, also the training business has just changed moderately and has barely adapted. We are still exercising intensity, procedures, consistency concerning passing, paths and so on. Football is played as ever, no matter how this game is interpreted. Nevertheless, we are struggling with this simple change.

Which changes do you mean?

My impatience, my obstinacy searches for something to adhere to. I feel something, but I can't put it into words yet! Does it perceive something, followed by the decision, followed by the implementation? In the end, my actions during the match are bound to these three factors and steps. On closer inspection, they are responsible for good or bad, for successful or less successful play. And returning to the mentioned question concerning the modification of training, here is the definite announcement: This is to be exercised in the youth sector.

Back to match observation or, better, to the theme of observation once again. What exactly do we perceive and what do we ascertain in the end?

Against Team B, Team A experienced this, what we are experiencing against every opponent at the moment: One Team (B) just tries to maintain the result and to prevent a goal against them with all their might, the other team (A), which feels called upon as the fancied team because of their situation, for example as the home team, higher rated in the table, because of the history, and so on, struggles with creating the game. Any deficiencies of the idea, the "Why" and subsequently the "How," are revealed relentlessly while playing with the ball and frequently, it is just negligence of the opponent, thus sensible errors of Team B, which let chances arise.

If the same team (A) has to compete against us now, it is situated in front of its own goal area with ten players and grows beyond itself at every counter. It is an easy game for them against us because it needs neither an idea of creating the game—the "Why" and "How"—nor does it put its back into the game and is nevertheless able to win everything with one action! We should be aware of this if we look at these matches and if we want to gain knowledge for the clash with us. We will find this, which is expecting us, Team Germany, just very partly in these matches—but much more likely in the underdog (B) than in the supposed favorite (A)!

This sounds logical. What should Team A, the 'good one,' take into account in this case?

We've come full circle. Just the "good one" can find a solution. The less "good one" only joins in! Another fact is that the sport of football has changed to the effect that at the level Germany joins the ranks, the "good one" doesn't only mark himself off from the "less good one," but that just the "good one" is able to give the game deciding stimuli. Only if we perceive these solutions in the trend observation, we can draw conclusions from this which type of player, which array and tactical alignment is suitable for the solution!

Is it a problem then that the game strategy of good teams will become transparent?

Of course, the game of former top teams has become so transparent that deficiencies—not having acknowledged or accepted the development—can be compensated not only with more force, more stamina and more technique. Keywords such as speed and efficiency mixed with lots of creativity: this is the recipe to success, the general response! But how does one acquire these skills?

For me this seems to be too simple and too easy! And then I recall Franz Beckenbauer's words: 'go out there, play football and score goals! ("geht's raus und spielts Fußball und schießt Tore!") We need to ask ourselves: What do I perceive? Which decisions do we make? And we need to know that everybody perceives and makes decisions, but everybody follows a different realization. Not all of them can be followed at the same time!

Do you have an example for us?

The best example for me at hand is Team Brazil! If there hadn't been any changes in football, then Brazil would still be the measure of all things in football. For there are hardly better and technically more talented football players than Brazilians. When we perceive these changes during game observation, then we can draw conclusions from this, see solutions and we know how to train this change. How should coaching be handled? When we see solutions, we can express these by knowing—not only intuitively—which player is suitable for this solution. Aspects, which have been forgotten during the development of football.

How can these perspectives be summarized?

This is how I pose the question and regarding Team Brazil not since yesterday: why does Team Brazil have so many difficulties keeping up? Why do the U-Teams everywhere else wake up from a bad dream? The aim everywhere is set high and stated with belief and certainty. Indeed, but why? Is the answer "we've had a bad day" sufficient? The game, the interpretation and own actions adds to the perception of changes, speaking about solutions preemptively and wanting and being able to train them—keyword coaching.

It is not the absolute stars, which possess these abilities, or have acquired them during their career. There are two, three, four players that are a good example for an appropriate game understanding: Diego Godín, central defender of Atlético Madrid. During game initiation from defense to offense he has a very good choice of position. He recognizes the area in which one has to stand and be free and initiator for offense.

Or Busquets from FC Barcelona, who can read, recognize, and sense his own team's game and the opponent's game very well as a defensive midfielder and who is thus almost always at the right place. Michael Bradley of Team USA, who has an excellent and very diverse repertoire of actions. He invests a lot of running time in his game, is game designer and completes the actions, as he also goes into the box. Miro Klose, a center forward, who thinks and collaborates! He always knew where his opponent was standing or not. He had a feel for where his opponent was looking for a solution and where he did not find any!

How could we understand and accept the huge change in football? The change—paradigm shift—in the realization. Change in efficiency. How can investors, fans and spectators watch and at the same time comprehend this sport?

I will return to the origin of the game with this question. The game with the ball and the foot on an amateur football field. The center of this sport is about having joy in the game, scoring goals, as many and as often as possible. This is the basic idea and the tactics. However, these simple key points are so extremely difficult to transfer to successful actions on the field and to train them.

References

Biermann, C. (2015). THEMEN: Spielanalyse, Taktik. *11 Freunde*, 160.

Grunz, A., Memmert, D. & Perl, J. (2012). Tactical pattern recognition in soccer games by means of special self-organizing maps. *Human Movement Science, 31*, 334–43.

Memmert, D., Raabe, D., Knyazev, A., Franzen, A., Zekas, L., Rein, R., . . . Weber, H. (2016a). Big Data im Profi-Fußball. Analyse von Positionsdaten der Fußball-Bundesliga mit neuen innovativen Key Performance Indikatoren. *Leistungssport*, 1–13.

Memmert, D., Raabe, D., Knyazev, A., Franzen, A., Zekas, L., Rein, R., . . . Weber, H. (2016b). Innovative Leistungsindikatoren im Profifußball auf Basis von Positionsdaten. *Impulse, 2*, 14–21.

Memmert, D. & Rein, R. (2018, in press). Match analysis, Big Data and tactics: current trends in elite soccer. *German Journal of Sport Medicine*.

2

A HISTORICAL PERSPECTIVE ON POSITIONAL DATA

Football tactics: as old as the game itself

Anyone who loves football or has even played him-/herself knows how simple the game is. Two teams of eleven players each, one ball and the common goal to score more goals than the opponent. This simplicity is one of the main reasons why the sport enjoys such a great popularity all over the world. And although the rules of the game can be explained in three lines—perhaps even for that reason— it spreads an unrivalled fascination. We don't only like to play. We also love to watch others while they play, we talk shop about the philosophy of the game and enjoy its unique aesthetics that arises when 22 players chase the ball. It is not without reason that since the birth of "the beautiful game" people are discussing the question of what attractive football is supposed to look like.

Anyone who has also started to think about football will have discovered—in addition to its beauty—an incredible complexity. A complexity characterised by movement patterns, match plans and playing philosophies, but also of creativity (Memmert, 2011, 2015). Nowadays, we are able to understand the mechanisms of the game with a previously unknown depth. This is possible due to newest technical developments, as well as a wealth of experience collected over the last decades. A century-long history precedes the dissemination of automated match analysis—the most modern form of performance diagnostics and central issue of this book. This history was shaped by pioneers of sports science, weird inventions, and technical revolutions.

A glimpse into the history books shows that thinking about football is almost as old as the game itself. From early on, coaches and observers were concerned with the question of how to play the game to be successful. What we now understand by football tactics goes all the way back to the beginning of the sport, as the sports book author Jonathan Wilson notes. In his excellent book, *Inverting the Pyramid: The History of Football Tactics*, he describes in a highly entertaining manner combined with a lot of ingenuity the tactical development from the "mob game of medieval Britain" to the world's most successful coaches today (Wilson, 2008).

On November 30, 1872, the first international football match took place. The national teams of England and Scotland faced each other, whereby the latter was represented by the team of FC Queen's Park, as the Scottish Football Association would not be founded until the following year. The match at Hamilton Crescent, now a cricket ground in Glasgow, Scotland, ended with a goalless draw. Back then

. —WELL KICKED—

FIGURE 2.1A, B AND C Inernational match England vs. Scotland (30 November, 1872).

Source: *Historia del Fútbol* by William Ralston (1848–1911), published 1872.

DRIBBLING

SOFT FALLING, FORTUNATELY

FIGURE 2.1A, B AND C Continued

Source: *Historia del Fútbol* by William Ralston (1848–1911), published 1872.

the players already played roughly in what we today call a formation, which Wilson describes as a 1–2–7 on the English and 2–2–6 on the Scottish side.

Up to today's popular systems, which seem to be much more balanced in regard to the player's positions, tactics in football experienced a multitude of innovations. Concerning playing systems, which constantly adapted to current developments, strikers gradually moved back to the midfield and finally into the defense. This can be explained by changes in the rules as well as in the increasing professionalization and acceleration of the game.

Notepads and measuring instruments

Along with football tactics, the desire to make a player's performance tangible matured over the years. In analogy to the tactical ideas of legendary coaches like Herbert Chapman, the first approaches of what we today call the concept of match analysis emerged. In the absence of technical tools, at a time when the first commercial computers hadn't even been developed, old-fashioned tools were state-of-the-art: pen and paper. From the first incomprehensible scribbles of movements and passing combinations, so-called manual notation systems emerged—you can think of it as a kind of guide for the structured documentation of match games with set symbols and an elaborate grammar.

However, the beginnings of these hand notation systems are not to be found in football, but in baseball—the sport which is responsible for many other

FIGURE 2.2 The American Hugh Fullerton, first game analyst in baseball

Source: The A. G. Spalding Baseball Collection

FIGURE 2.3 The American Lloyd Messersmith in 1930.

Source: DePauw University Archives and Special Collections

revolutions in match analysis, as we will find out later. Already in 1912, the American Hugh Fullerton published a twelve-page essay in the *American Magazine* in which he divided the baseball field into several zones and analyzed the success probabilities of more than 10,000 balls hit in these zones (Fullerton, 1912). Although science was involved in sports at various levels at that time already, the well-known sports journalist Fullerton was the first one to write an article about the systematic elaboration of match statistics.

Shortly after, scientists from other sports started to develop standardized systems with which matches could be annotated. With uniform terms and predefined schemes, they were able to break down the complex gameplay onto single moves and also to catalog the actions of the players. The gathered information allowed not only for evaluation, but also to compare between multiple matches.

One of the very first hand notation systems in sports was developed by the American Lloyd Messersmith around 1930 (Lyons, 1996, cf. Figure 2.3). The main focus of this multi-talented physical education teacher and coach was basketball, baseball, and American football. Apart from the documentation of match actions, Messersmith also dealt with the physical performance of athletes during the competition. Together with his colleagues, he developed a "tracking-apparatus," which allowed measurement of the running distance covered by a single player.

This self-made electrical device consisted of a miniature pitch, a needle to record the location of the player on the field, an electric pulse counter, and a large wooden battery box. It had to be operated by two people: while one person traced the running distance of the player on the adjustable pad, the second person wrote down the output of the pulse counter. Already in 1931, this fancy invention was able to estimate how many kilometers the center in a basketball game reeled off on average. According to Messersmith, it was around 5.5 km (all centers of one team together), at least in college basketball between 1931 and 1941.

Twenty years ahead of his time

Some years later, football found its first match analyst as well: the Briton Charles Reep, a passionate and controversial personality. Reep was born in 1904 in Torpoint, a small English town in the southwestern County of Cornwall (Pollard, 2002). Already in his youth he developed an interest in football and regularly attended the matches of neighboring club Plymouth Argyle. After qualifying as an accountant he joined the Royal Air Force (RAF), which he left in 1955 as a lieutenant colonel. During his time with the RAF, he met Charles Jones who was by then captain of Arsenal (London) and coached by Herbert Chapman. In 1933, Jones was invited to give a talk at Reep's base. Inspired by his speeches about Arsenal's wing play, Reep began to deal intensively with football tactics. Whenever he was able to spare some time from his duties at the RAF, he visited a match between the two north London clubs, Arsenal and Tottenham Hotspur, and meticulously studied their attacking game. Subsequently, he applied his findings and reflections to some of the RAF teams which he coached.

The start of his career as a match analyst took place in spring 1950 during a match between Swindon Town and Bristol Rovers. Reep spontaneously pulled out his notebook during the match and started to capture what he saw with written symbols and notes. From this point, he was hooked on his new hobby. By the end of the year he had developed a complete notation system, and a year later he had begun to produce weekly match reports for Wolverhampton Wanderers (Wolves)—as a consultant for manager Stan Cullis, under whom Wolves became one of the dominant clubs in England in the early 1950s. Three years later he moved on to Sheffield Wednesday, followed by further posts.

Reep's hobby remained his profession until his death in 2002. Already in 1968 he had analyzed almost 2,500 games using his system—an impressive number of matches and a huge dataset. He eventually published the results of his analyses, together with Bertrand Benjamin, in the *Journal of the Royal Statistical Society* (Reep & Benjamin, 1968). Among other things, he concluded that 80per cent of all goals were scored after three or fewer passes had been made. He also calculated that half of the goals were scored after the ball was regained in the opponent's half, as well as an average ratio of 10:1 between shots and goals. These numbers would remain constant in Reep's further publications.

Backed up by his analyses, Reep consolidated his conviction that the direct game utilizing long passes (also called the *long ball game, direct play*, or *route one football*) is the most promising way to play successfully. And he was not alone— other scientists followed and confirmed his results in their work. Reep went on and gained approval in non-academic circles as well. Among others, Charles Hughes, later Director of Coaching of the British Football Association, met with Reep in 1981 for personal instruction.

Nevertheless, the story of Charles Reep is not an immaculate tale of a data junkie who revolutionized the sport, as it would be done by Bill James years later. Already during his active time, Reep was not always appreciated. And also posthumously he has been criticized again and again for his undifferentiated approach—among others by the aforementioned Wilson. Not without good reason, since his central doctrine of the three-pass rule came along with a decisive shortcoming: Reep was right about the fact that most goals resulted from short pass combinations, but he ignored the fact that in a regular football match, sequences with fewer passes were becoming much more frequent than those with more passes. His results consisted only of absolute frequencies and were not an appropriate measure for effectiveness.

In fact, if one considers the success rates of passing outcomes with respect to the frequency of their occurrence, it becomes clear that actions involving three or fewer passes lead far less frequently to a goal major—a misinterpretation of his findings and symbolic of the somewhat simple models which Reep developed over the years; let alone the advantages of a playing style involving much ball possession and long passing combinations resulting in increased fatigue levels of the opponent, which he did not even consider.

In retrospect, it is difficult to determine whether Reep's view of successful football was the result of incorrect analyses or whether he tried to reinforce his biased ideas with crude mathematics. Nevertheless, he influenced English football. Over decades, Charles Hughes anchored Reep's results in the curricula of the Football Association. Thus, English football was shaped by a game of longer passes—a fact that can still be seen today in the lower leagues; a development in which Reep and his analyses played an important role. At the same time, he was 20 years ahead of his colleagues in the field of match analysis. He developed the first-hand notation system specifically for football and showed an extraordinary passion in what he did. He spent up to 80 hours evaluating the match reports produced in the stadium. Even if his achievements in the game of football remain controversial, his place as the first match analyst in history is undisputed.

The science of paper and pencil

Little is known about the system developed by Reep, but over the years other systems have continually emerged and had begun to capture more and more detail on the field. It was recognized quickly that scenes in the offensive third of the field were crucial for goal-scoring opportunities. Furthermore, the early and late match analysts were always curious about *where* on the field the actions took place. Like pioneer Hugh Fullerton, analysts started to divide the field into zones and developed fine grid fields to locate events of note. Even today, these so-called grid field analyses, better known as heat maps, are a popular tool to visualize the locations of players. The meaningfulness of these pretty graphics may be discussed, but it shows the need for and the importance of not only capturing results quantitatively, but also conveying the information to the viewer in an appealing manner.

Yet, the Scottish scientist A. H. Ali carried this to extremes. He had also developed a hand notation system with which he specifically wanted to examine the attacking behavior of a team in the top Scottish league (Ali, 1986). Armed with paper and pencil, he watched 18 games from the main stand in the late 1980s and documented every single attack. He sketched his diagrams on prepared drawings of the pitch that he had overlayed with a grid. After the games he labeled every play with X and Y coordinates—a kind of analog predecessor of the positional data as we know them today. His results, however, lagged behind the complexity of his methods: For the team he was investigating, Ali concluded that attacks down the wings were the most effective while long passes mostly ended up as offside.

Moving into the digital era

Although hand notation systems were the gold standard over decades and their extensive use established the first knowledge base in football, they had two distinct deficiencies: not only were the systems difficult to learn for novices and a certain period of familiarization was needed, but the process of recording was also enormously time consuming. Per game, several hours had to be spent recording and archiving all actions (Pollard, Reep, & Hartley, 1988). This would drastically change over the course of the 1990s due to increasingly available technical tools.

In this decade, game analysis became almost completely digitalized (Reilly, 2003). Although many scouts and observers still worked with handwritten notes at the beginning of the new millennium—and they still do today—almost everyone enters these into the computer or feeds the information into a database at the end of the day. Especially the recording of match data has only become digital since the beginning of the 21st century.

First, data entry into the computer was revolutionized, which greatly accelerated the collection of match information. Already in 1987 the scientists Church and Hughes developed so-called Concept Keyboards (Church & Hughes, 1987) (at the same time a similar technology with the name Playpad became popular in Canada), a special keyboard which had specific keys for game actions such as passes and saves by the goalkeeper. A rapid acceleration compared to the tedious insertion of observed actions.

Data entry was even faster with so-called speech recognition systems, which came on the market a few years later and made keyboards redundant. What was seen on the field was spoken in a predefined code into a microphone while at the same time the location of the action was marked on a virtual field on the screen.

Also, the integration of stationary video sources became technically feasible (e.g., Franks & Nagelkerke, 1988). In Germany, Winkler was the first to try to

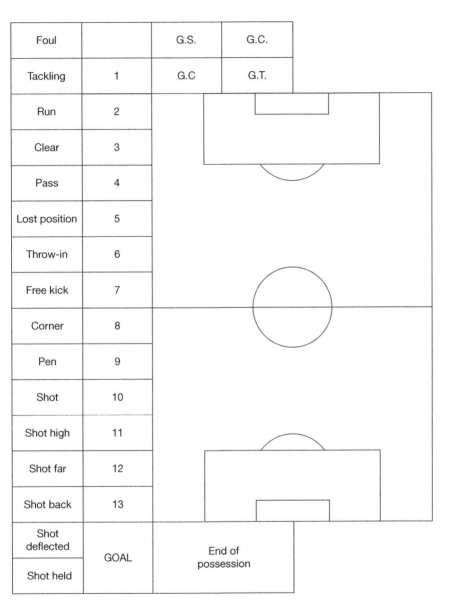

Foul		G.S.	G.C.
Tackling	1	G.C	G.T.
Run	2		
Clear	3		
Pass	4		
Lost position	5		
Throw-in	6		
Free kick	7		
Corner	8		
Pen	9		
Shot	10		
Shot high	11		
Shot far	12		
Shot back	13		
Shot deflected	GOAL	End of possession	
Shot held			

FIGURE 2.4 The so-called "Concept Keyboard" for data input in notation analysis in football.

Source: Re-sketched by Hughes et al. (1988)

make the whole game visible on the video screen by using two cameras (Winkler, 1989). This is the only possible way to adequately assess the quality of long passes as well as the interaction between attacking and defensive players. Nowadays, video sources that cover the entire pitch are available for almost all top leagues.

In the following years, analysts started to encode information with time stamps and linked these to the match videos so that mouse-clicks sufficed to access scenes based on match information or filters. Due to increasingly powerful processors, video analysis was finally transferred from the VHS recorder to the computer. With the help of software packages for behavioral analysis, analysts were now able to tag video sequences, assigning keywords to each game scene in order to organize them more accurately. To date, video analysis is a crucial part of the everyday work of every match analyst, and is now widespread. Apart from the top leagues, even youth team matches are now being recorded on video by service providers—for example all matches of the under-17 and under-19 Bundesliga teams in Germany.

Video analysis was also used systematically in Germany in the 2001–2002 season for match post-processing by the Institute for Sports and Sports Science of the University of Heidelberg, under the direction of the main author in the context of a cooperation with TSG Hoffenheim (Memmert, 2006, 2014). At that time, the club still played in the *Regionalliga Süd* (4th tier in German football). In cooperation with Flick/Schön (TSG Hoffenheim), arrangements were made regarding analyses of the home matches of the respective clubs. Prior to that season, tags were predefined to select relevant game scenes.

FIGURE 2.5 Hansi Flick and Alfred Schön; game analysis with dictation machine in Hoffenheim, 2001

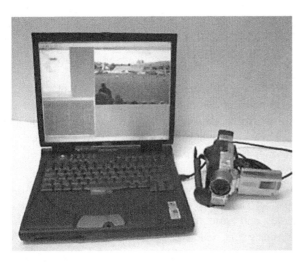

FIGURE 2.6 Game analysis software PosiCap, distributed by the company Master-Coach

During home matches, the respective assistant coach's job was to mark crucial and important scenes with tags online. For this purpose, they recorded the respective abbreviations positive/offensive, positive/defensive, negative/offensive, and negative/defensive onto a dictation machine. The coach's four possible distributions—a 4-field scheme—defined match actions, wherein the home team was always the focus of interest.

With the referee blowing the starting whistle (synchronization mark), the team from the Sport Institute simultaneously recorded the games on video in their own stadium. The trainers finally received video sections of approximately 10 minutes each, showing important selected match scenes of the latest home fixture.

When Ralf Rangnick subsequently became manager of 1899 Hoffenheim, all of the *Regionalliga* (!) teams were extensively recorded on video for pre-match preparation and subsequently evaluated with the analysis program PosiCap, distributed by the company Master-Coach. Nowadays, there are numerous providers worldwide offering match analyses for team and racket sports.

The origin of video analysis can thereby also be linked to a North American. The Canadian Roger Paul Neilson, born 1934 in Toronto, was probably the first manager to introduce systematic video analyses to professional sports. He dedicated himself to ice hockey, and in his long career he coached numerous clubs of the National Hockey League, including the Peterborough Petes, the Toronto Maple Leafs, and the New York Rangers. He was known for his devotion and affinity to innovation and thus presented videos to his players with home game scenes long before many other teams and was therefore given the nickname "Captain Video." By his death in 2003, video analysis in many sports had spread worldwide.

INTERVIEW WITH PROFESSOR DR. LAMES, SPORTS SCIENTIST AT TU MUNICH

Team and racket sport research is by now also an integral part of sport science worldwide. Developments of computer systems for match analyses or algorithmic evaluations of match data are established elements of the academic world. We have talked to Professor Dr. Martin Lames on how exactly research at universities has taken on board the tactical aspects of football over the past few years.

Professor Lames finished his Ph.D. on simulative performance diagnostics in tennis in 1989, at Johannes Gutenberg University Mainz with the Ph.D. supervisors Manfred Letzelter and Jürgen Perl. The habilitation was in 1997 at Christian-Albrechts-University Kiel, followed by professorial positions at University Rostock (1996) and Augsburg (2003). Since 2009 he has been chair of the Institute for Training Sciences and Sport Informatics at TU Munich.

Dear Professor Lames, when was the birth of match analysis as a research field at universities in Germany?

Even if one can speak neither of a "birth" nor of "match analysis," one can see the first approaches in the direction of scientific match analysis in Germany at the DHfK in Leipzig. Its Institute of Team and Racket Sports was led by Hugo Döbler. Stiehler published the first publications on methodologies of systematic game observation in 1962. The work of Köhler in 1967 is another cornerstone, with which the substantial performance diagnostic tasks of match analysis were formulated at a very early point. Already back then he knew that it was important to mathematically solve the complex character of match performance with the development of a formula on calculating the performance coefficient, and thus he initiated the search for KPIs as early as 1967.

In the West, the first performance diagnostic approaches for team and racket sports were made by Hagedorn in 1971. Conceptionally one can already find here the complete process chain, beginning with system development up to the transfer to training. Historically also very interesting is the project by Andresen, Brettschneider, and Hagedorn in 1977, with which a then newly invented PC from Nixdorf, Paderborn, was used for the registration of actions in basketball using a barcode scanner.

And abroad?

Internationally the American "Stats" approaches in Baseball go back to the late 19th century. According to statements from American colleagues, the stats were taken care of by the media and the fans for a long time and have more and more developed into a lucrative line of business. Only a short while ago the training and competition control based on match analyses came to the foreground as a genuine field of application. Today stats and match analysis form an intensive synthesis, which grants the American high-class sports a leading position in technology.

Worth mentioning is also the group by led Mike Hughes in Cardiff, UK, who stood out from the Thomas Reilly School at John Moores University in Liverpool and who focused especially on objective feedback for coaches regarding game events. His match observation approach, Notational Analysis (see above) was developed more or less simultaneously to that in Germany. However, till the late 1990s neither an exchange nor any contact took place.

Which developments in the universities followed from that time until now?

Here it is difficult to do justice to all developments, as match analysis with the increasing technological possibilities has become a widely and internationally renowned field of work. Absolutely noteworthy though is the TESSY working group under Jürgen Perl, who explicitly focused on "sport informatics" starting in the mid-1980s in Mainz. His group created sophisticated hardware developments for match analysis, such as data base and video connection, voice input, location entries via digitalization boards, and software developments such as expert systems, information systems, or classification with neuronal networks. My own dissertation of 1989 on simulative performance diagnostics and my monography on systematic game observation of 1994 are probably just as noteworthy as the practice-oriented contributions of the Institute for Sport Games at the German Sports University, for example by Prof. Weber.

How did scientific research react to the introduction of positional data?

The availability of positional data constituted a decisive point. At first this key moment was experimentally realized at the turn of the millennium, then in academic projects such as projects by Beetz and the author at TU Munich and the University Augsburg, and finally with large resource support by commercial providers. With this, the search phase, not yet finalized, of appropriate evaluations and of a methodological securing of practice-oriented data generation began.

Which were the central subjects at the national and international symposia? Which subjects were especially discussed among the experts?

At an early stage, the ever-growing amount of data directed the focus toward appropriate evaluation methods. The distinction between match analyses for theoretical and practical purposes, which differ in design, sample, method, and objective, is a landmark—see my research works with Tim McGarry from

Canada or the DFG projects of colleagues Perl and Memmert, for example. Ever new concepts, for instance from the theory of dynamic systems, are applied in order to capture the nature of sports. In the practical arena, it was recognized soon that a naive "the-more-the-better" is not applicable for the assessment of the variables of positional analyses in football (as, for example, running scope and intensity).

So, all that glisters is not gold?

The search for more practical indicators started here as well, which are just able to claim reputably to depict partial aspects of the game. Therefore, they should not be allocated the buzzwords "Key Performance Indicators," which come originally from economics. In the English-speaking area, a *practical impact debate* can be observed, which searches for more appropriate ways of match analysis for practical purposes, based on the determination that previous scientific investigations have little effect on established training, whereby qualitative methods are an issue as well.

At a bound: What are your conclusions on the present scientific developments in match analysis despite the above points of criticism?

Altogether, match analysis represents a dynamic and increasingly prosperous field of application in sport science, considering the wide range of international conferences and variety of the topics that are covered there.

The birth of X–Y

Like other developments, positional data, as used today, are a child of the digitization of football. In contrast to other data sources, their development was not only accelerated by the technological progress but was recently made possible by it. Indeed, there were analysts, such as Ali, who still drew moves in a coordinate system by hand (Ali, 1986). Yet, the history of development of data is an interaction of innovations in the areas of software and hardware.

A particularly creative pilot project was carried out by scientists in the Belgian region of Flandern in 1984 (Van Gool, Van Gerven, & Boutmans, 1988). The researchers placed a film camera on one of the surrounding high-rise buildings at a friendly match between the teams of the Catholic University of Leuven and the University of Birmingham, from which they could record the entire pitch on 16 mm film. From a height of 57 meters and at five frames per second, they filmed the entire 7–0 home win by the Belgians. Nevertheless, the recording of the match from a bird's eye perspective was not made in order to analyze the match with conventional video analysis. Instead, with a little ingenuity, they subsequently managed to extract the first positional dataset in history from their film.

To do so, they projected the recordings onto a X–Y coordinate system and digitized the picture with the help of a *Mutoh Drafting and Digitization Machine CX 3000*. The dataset, stored on floppy disks, served to examine the physical performances of seven selected players. Additionally, their heart rate had been measured during the 90 minutes at regular intervals. In summary, the Belgian scientists were able to show at which intensity the average 10.2 kilometers were run by the players, and correlate the results with heart rate and oxygen absorption.

The commercial start of "Player Tracking Technologies," as they are known today, happened about 10 years after these somewhat improvised pioneer attempts. The French company Amisco developed a first market-ready system in 1996, which initially used thermal cameras to locate the athletes.

In 1998, the French national team used this system in preparation for the FIFA World Cup in their home country (Castellano, Alvarez-Pastor, & Bradley, 2014). The French company's greatest rival in those days came from England. At least off the pitch, as the company Prozone, operating from Leeds since 1995, entered the market with a similar system. On the pitch, the picture looked a little different in 1998: while France clinched the title, England had failed in the round of 16 against Argentina.

Amisco and Prozone merged in 2011, both companies had provided their camera systems to most of the top European leagues over a number of years. Four years later, in May 2015, the American data giant STATS pur-chased the tracking provider, who had advanced as a global player and whose databanks created the profiles of over 100,000 players and 12,000 events per year. In general, the development has accelerated enormously especially in recent years. The list of tracking system providers is long and changes almost monthly due to acquisitions and merges. At the same time, the volume of produced data rises rapidly, as almost every top club draws on this new data source even for training.

Besides classical camera tracking, which meanwhile has switched from thermal to HD cameras, further technologies used for the acquisition of positional data have been regularly established. These include radar-based systems or GNSS devices, which can be worn by the players. Both methods have developed parallel to the camera systems recent years up to market saturation.

Military research as well lent a helping hand as these technologies emerged. In one example, tracking technologies based on radar engineering profited from the investigation of different missile guidance systems. GNSS transponders, which work with the help of satellites, frequently collaborate with the American satellite system GPS. The system for location determination developed from the US Ministry of Defense had been restricted to the non-military use until the turn of the millennium. To avoid misuse, the signals delivered were layered by artificial noise, but from 2000 this precaution was turned off so that there was no longer any obstacle to its utilization in sports. A detailed description of the various techniques is given in the following chapter.

Screenshot taken from a scouting analysis program during a match between England and Mexico

German	English translation
Markierung hinzufügen	Add marker
Start Seq.	Start sequence
Videozeit	Time of video
Match clock Eintrag	Match clock entry
Clock nutzen	Use clock
Speicherplatz für Videoaufnahme	Memory capacity for video recording

FIGURE 2.7 Screenshot of the PosiCap surface

On the way to complete automation

Closely linked to and a constant catalyst of the development of modern tracking technologies were the noticeable advancements made in the area of software during recent years. Breakthroughs in the field of image processing were of crucial importance, making it possible to reliably extract individual players and their movements from several combined camera perspectives. Today, algorithms for recognizing persons or faces in (moving) images find application in numerous fields of technology.

In addition, complex algorithms form the basis for analyzing the collected information. Without elaborate processing and evaluation of datasets, their value for sports is close to zero. With the right models, on the other hand, it is possible to automate computer-assisted match analysis so that complex calculations are even available live during the match.

In the North American area the development of software solutions for analyses was initially connected to research that was, among others, promoted by the American Department of Defense. By 2001 American researchers tried to classify different attacking variations in American Football taken from video recordings of the New England Patriots (Intille & Bobick, 2001). The idea behind the study was to automatically recognize and describe movement patterns of groups of agents.

In general, physical aspects were initially the center of attention in the first studies based on positional data in football; however, tactics have recently become more and more important. To draw conclusions regarding tactical behavior from the available information, complex algorithms are required that we will examine more thoroughly in the second part of this book.

Yet to reach this point, a few obstacles had to be overcome. At the beginning of scientific observation of football tactics with the help of positional data, by the end of 2000 the availability of large datasets at universities was scarce. Not everybody who wanted was able to gain access to the new datasets. The coordination of theory and practice still had to be established, but necessity is the mother of invention. Thus some scientists took the initiative and found alternatives. While some typed player coordinates taken from video recordings into the computer, others used virtual football simulations derived from game consoles.

Others used data taken from robot football, of which two variations are known: In the "real" version either human-like, so-called humanoid robots, stand opposite each other on a miniature pitch, or rather small, moving machines take, transport and throw the ball. The second version is fully virtual and simulated on computer: eleven machines stand opposite to each other on a virtual field, their physical behavior copied from the originals.

The main idea behind competitions such as the annual RoboCup is the promotion of intelligent algorithms for multi-agent control. When watching internet videos of the rather hectic virtual mini-players, one will at least recognize a rudimentary similarity to the game on grass, even regarding tactics. Whether this suffices to derive performance indicators for high-class football remains an open question.

Nevertheless in recent years good data sources have become more accessible for scientists. There are still smaller, technical problems with particular systems that need to be tackled when recording positional data, but finding a solution currently seems to be just a matter of time. In the coming years further progress regarding accuracy and availability can be expected. Right now there is an even more exciting question: How will the algorithmic processing of captured data progress in the coming years? For only the intelligent utilization of data masses will reveal the full potential of this new chapter of data analysis.

FIGURE 2.8A AND B Examples of humanoid robots

Source: Ralf Roletschek/roletschek.at, image licensed under the GNU Free Documentation License and the Creative Commons Attribution 3.0 Unported license.

INTERVIEW WITH GERMANY'S FIRST COMPUTER SCIENTIST IN SPORTS, PROF. DR. JÜRGEN PERL

In our digital era, the integration of IT techniques in sports is not a phenomenon exclusively emerging in the realm of football analyses. Ever since the 1980s sport informatics is constantly growing as a scientific field located the interface between sport and digital technologies and can safely be regarded as a substantive subarea of sports science.

One of its founding fathers in Germany is Prof. Dr. em. Jürgen Perl, founder and first president of the International Association of Computer Science in Sport (IACSS), as well as founder of the section sport informatics of the German Association of Sport Sciences. He developed the match analysis tool SOCCER© among others, which is used in many case studies presented in this book. In an interview we talked to him about his research areas, the history of automatized game analysis, and the latest developments in the field of positional data.

Prof. Dr. Perl, you hold a doctorate in mathematics and informatics granted by the universities of Osnabrück and Mainz and have especially worked in the field of sport informatics, among others with the German Association of Sport Sciences (dvs) and the IACSS. Which research areas are your central ones nowadays?

My central research areas are generally model formation and simulation, medical informatics, as well as sport informatics. My emphasis lies in physiologic performance analysis, with the development of the product family PerPot, and on pattern and match analysis with the help of neuronal networks with the product family DyCoN.

You significantly participated in the development of automated game analysis. Can you give us a brief overview of the general history of automated match analysis in Germany? When and where did this start?

Match analysis started roughly in 1980 by Hagedorn, who delivered first approaches for the collection and analysis of match data in basketball based on online observations. In our collaboration we developed a video-based match analysis in basketball. In the next step I developed a video-based match analysis system for tactical pattern optimization in badminton, after which the video based tennis match analysis system TeSSy was developed in 1985 during cooperation with Miethling. This system was then expanded onto the sport games squash, volleyball, basketball, and handball, as well as the martial arts wrestling and fencing.

How did the development of automated game analysis continue?

Since 1990 rule-based systems (grammars) have been developed for the description and simulation of actions and interactions in racket sports, team sports, and martial arts. Furthermore, we presented first approaches for the use of neuronal networks to recognize process patterns and tactical patterns. To be then able to analyze even small, dynamically changing datasets, I developed the dynamically learning network type DyCoN.

First productive DyCoN analyses succeeded at about 1995 in volleyball together with Lames, as well as in handball with Pfeiffer. Miethling and I were also able to generate TeSSY variations for behavior analysis according to "soft" data in tennis. Based on this we were able to change the TeSSy family to digital video data since the turn of the millennium and we were thus also able to expand these to a complete system including automatic analysis, data base and simulation.

Which further developments have occurred since 2000?

Together with Memmert the first approaches for behavior and process analysis in football were developed, whereby the fundamental analysis goals were creativity recognition and simulation. Starting 2005, the cooperation with Dr. Memmert continued regarding the development of network based and process oriented analysis methods for football, especially with the development of concepts of formation patterns. Tilp and I then transferred the formation pattern approach to handball.

What have been the latest developments since 2010?

At last, automatically generated positional data was available for football. Furthermore I developed the analysis program SOCCER as a modular extendable complete system for various analysis concepts, methods and functionalities. Since last year Memmert and I are concentrating on the analysis of complex processes and the development of process based KPIs.

When were the first activities regarding the above-mentioned automatic positional data recognition?

These activities go back to the year 1989, in the context of the first workshop for sport and informatics in Hochheim, as the intention declaration of the Fraunhofer-Institute Nürnberg for tennis. First approaches for the collection of positioning data in football by the Fraunhofer-Institute Nürnberg can be dated after 2000, with the development of secondary radar for player registration and a chip for ball registration.

Was the use of robot football and simulation in field studies able to deliver important findings for positional data and match analysis?

In the time between 1995 till approximately 2005, robot football (RoboCup, see above) was a central subject in the areas of game simulation and robotics. Tournaments and specific work group activities sponsored by the computer industry caused rapid initial success. However, they also quickly revealed possibility limits and the actual goals of industrial use: tactical and technical abilities of football robots are and remain minimalistic.

Was match analysis and simulation also observed in this program?

Match analysis and simulation without robots were part of the program, but they were not supported. The orientation was rather in the development of human like robot movements and robot interaction, with the goal of a "social" robot. In the past five years we have come closer to this goal.

Do first advanced studies regarding the use of positional data for game analysis in football exist today?

Yes, these have initially been documented since approximately 2005, and since 2010 with the help of SOCCER.

References

Ali, A. H. (1986). A statistical analysis of tactical movement patterns in soccer. In T. Reilly, A. Lees, K. Davids, & W. J. Murphy (Eds.). *Science and football* (pp. 302–308). London: E. & F.N. Spon.

Castellano, J., Alvarez-Pastor, D., & Bradley, P. S. (2014). Evaluation of research using computerised tracking systems (Amisco® and Prozone®) to analyse physical performance in elite soccer: A systematic review. *Sports Medicine, 44*(5), 701–712.

Church, S. & Hughes, M. (1987, April). *Patterns of play in association football—a computerised analysis*. Communication to First World Congress of Science and Football, Liverpool (pp. 13–17).

Franks, I. M. & Nagelkerke, P. (1988). The use of computer interactive video in sport analysis. *Ergonomics, 31*(11), 1593–1603.

Fullerton, H. S. (1912). The inside game: The science of baseball. *The American Magazine, 70*, 2–13.

Hughes, M. D., Robertson, K., & Nicholson, A. (1988). Comparison of patterns of play of successful amd unsuccessful teams in the 1986 World Cup for soccer. In T. Reilly, A. Lees, K. Davids, & W. Murphy (Eds.). *Science and football* (pp. 363–367). London: E. & F.N. Spon.

Intille, S. S. & Bobick, A. F. (2001). Recognizing planned, multiperson action. *Computer Vision and Image Understanding, 81*(3), 414–445.

Lyons, K. (1996). Lloyd Messersmith. In M. Hughes (ed.) *Notational Analysis of Sport—I & II*, 49–59.

Memmert, D. (2006, 2014). *Optimales Taktiktraining im Leistungsfußball*. Balingen: Spitta Verlag.

Memmert D. (2011). Sports and creativity. In M. A. Runco & S. R. Pritzker (Eds.). *Encyclopedia of creativity* (pp. 373–378). San Diego: Academic Press.

Memmert, D. (2015). *Teaching tactical creativity in team and racket sports: Research and practice.* Abingdon, UK: Routledge.

Pollard, R. (2002). Charles Reep (1904–2002): Pioneer of notational and performance analysis in football. *Journal of Sports Sciences, 20*(10), 853–855.

Pollard, R., Reep, C., & Hartley, S. (1988). The quantitative comparison of playing styles in soccer. In T. Reilly, A. Lees, K. Davids, & W. J. Murphy (Eds.). *Science and Football* (pp. 309–315). London: E. & F.N. Spon.

Reep, C. & Benjamin, B. (1968). Skill and chance in association football. *Journal of the Royal Statistical Society, Series A (General), 131*(4), 581–585.

Reilly, T. (2003). *Science and soccer* (pp. 252–264). London: Routledge.

Van Gool, D., Van Gerven, D., & Boutmans, J. (1988). The physiological load imposed on soccer players during real match-play. In T. Reilly, A. Lees, K. Davids, & W. J. Murphy (Eds.). *Science and Football* (pp. 51–59). London: E. & F.N. Spon.

Wilson, J. (2008). *Inverting the Pyramid: A History of Football Tactics.* Orion.

Winkler, W. (1989). Neue Wege in der Taktikschulung. *Fußballtraining,* 7(4), 46–50.

3

TECHNOLOGICAL BACKGROUND

The "Big Three" of player tracking technologies

Looking at the entire trajectory of a midfield player in the first half of an ordinary top-league match, as seen in Figure 3.1, it appears as an inscrutable mesh. From these raw data the match analysts will eventually draw their conclusions, but until then, a lot will happen with the data. The initial clump of movement does not appear very meaningful at first sight. One can roughly determine where on the pitch the player was operating, but nothing can be said about which role s/he took while doing so.

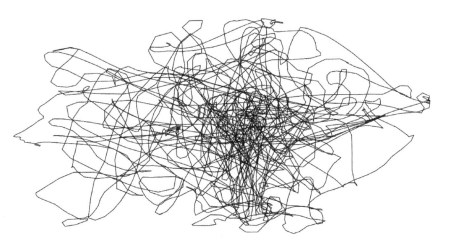

FIGURE 3.1 A midfielder's total running paths in the first half (45 minutes) of a regular Bundesliga match

FIGURE 3.2 Argentine international Lionel Messi, possibly the world's best player, surrounded by Chile's Alexis Sanchez, Gary Medel, Arturo Vidal, and Charles Aranguiz (2016)

Source: Don Emmert/AFP/Getty Images

Yet, before any analysis of those trajectories can be done, the question remains of how these raw data are acquired. If one of the world's best dribblers, such as Lionel Messi, starts another breathtaking solo, the path he takes appears inch-perfect on the analyst's laptop within seconds. To do so, the most advanced technical devices are used in combination with state-of-the-art methods of computer vision and image processing. Most of the technologies used today to track Messi's runs work on such a high level that they do not miss any turn or directional change. While not many defenders can stop him, even Messi himself is not fast enough for the computer.

The theory behind modern tracking technologies is enormous and could fill an entire book by itself. Therefore, we will just provide a rough introduction to the three major technologies that are being used before returning to the core intention of this book: What happens with the data.

To this end we spoke with Prof. Dr. Arnold Baca, who is an expert in the field of positional data analysis. He studied computer science at the Vienna University of Technology and obtained his Ph.D. in Technical Sciences in 1986. In 1997, he habilitated at the University of Vienna. In 2008, he was assigned as University Professor for Kinesiology with a focus on biomechanics and computer science in sports. He then became head of the Institute of Biomechanics/Movement Sciences and Computer Sciences in Sport at the Department of Sport Science. The former president of the International Association of Computer Science in Sport knows the development of different systems for the acquisition of the players' positions from its infancy. His research foci are in the field of ubiquitous computing in sports, in game and competition analysis, as well as in biomechanical movement analysis.

"In the beginning people relied on notational systems and the player's positions were recorded manually. The disadvantage was that this procedure was way too time-consuming," he explains. One can easily imagine how long it must have taken to plot the location of 22 players and the ball over the entire course of 90 minutes onto a 2D system.

Yet, a lot has changed since then. Various companies have positioned themselves on the market and have continuously developed improved systems to track athletes. According to Baca, the functionality of those systems can be grouped into three categories: "Currently, there are three different systems available: The ones based on GPS signals, the video-based systems that rely on image processing technologies, and finally systems based on radar and microwave technology." All three come with different advantages, but all of them also suffer from drawbacks.

GPS-based systems

The first-mentioned system, based on satellite navigation systems like GPS, which was developed by the US military, can be seen at the training grounds of almost

FIGURE 3.3 Pierre-Emerick Aubameyang and Sokratis of Borussia Dortmund wearing GPS-transponder chest belts during a summer training camp (2017)

Source: Alexandre Simoes/Borussia Dortmund/Getty Images

all professional football clubs these days. Also in the Bundesliga more and more clubs put their trust in this method for performance monitoring.

Regarding their functionality, the small tracking devices resemble the modern smartphones we use for navigation in everyday life. They especially convince in terms of simplicity: Just one transponder is required per player in order to gather the data. Additionally, another device is used that receives information from the devices, plus a charger that provides the batteries with electricity. For professional clubs, this means not only markedly reduced costs, but they save an enormous logistical effort as well.

Another advantage of GPS trackers arises from the sensor technology, which is additionally integrated in the devices. The transponder, which is mostly fixed to a chest strap, also collects a whole range of fitness data alongside the running data. Indeed, the players just wear a single technical device on their body, but the analyst receives a variety of information. The array of additional technique is enormous. Almost standardly a heart rate monitor (electrocardiogram) is deployed and, depending on the supplier, even the player's respiratory rate is monitored. With this information, it can be shown how great an athlete's real physical load looks like. Moreover, the current fitness level can be assessed to avoid injuries caused by fatigue. This technology will be explained later.

However, the applied sensor technology goes beyond the gathering of biometric data: In order to increase accuracy in the acquisition of the players' pathways, acceleration sensors (accelerometers), gyroscope instruments, and compasses are additionally deployed. Although these measurements capture quick turnarounds or collisions with other players in even more detail, they also reveal one deficiency —the accuracy of the positions.

While the player's movement sequences can be described excellently, information on the precise locations of movements is often inaccurate. According to Arnold Baca, this is one of three blind spots inherent in satellite systems: "A big disadvantage is that it just works outdoors and the utilization of GPS receivers is generally not allowed in competition. Furthermore, the accuracy is limited."

Video-based systems

In contrast, video-based systems operate without the need for additional electronics on the player's body. These are based instead on a combination of different camera perspectives, which are generated by a variety of video systems usually installed under the stadium roof. Modern methods of image processing identify the player on the video pictures, and their pathways can be tracked by combining the different perspectives.

According to Prof. Dr. Baca the big advantage is the following: "In contrast to GPS systems, the video based systems using methods of image processing are also applicable in competition and there is no need for sensor technology worn by the players. Nevertheless, the systems work rather semiautomatically and a manual intervention is necessary if the players' positions are covert or lost." In other words:

Most methods are admittedly capable of recognizing the players of both teams on the moving image, but do not usually reveal who is who on the screen.

Furthermore it becomes problematic if players cross the path of the ball or celebrate following a goal. Frequently, the assignment is lost and has to be readjusted. In addition, different weather conditions or illumination levels impede the recognition of the players by creating additional noise in the picture.

This disadvantage inhibits video-based systems from running fully automatically according to the current state of technology. Until accurate data can be provided, a follow-up is usually required. Baca is sure that there is indeed still growth potential for this technology: "The automatic tracking is improved steadily, for example by probability distributions of the players' location regarding their role."

Radar- and microwave-based systems

The third option for detecting the players' positions is offered by so-called "radar- or microwave-based systems," as Baca refers to them. Similar to GPS systems, athletes wear small transponder units attached to the body, stored in a chest strap or on the shin guards. Nevertheless, their location is not recorded by means of a satellite navigation system but rather directly in the stadium or training ground: several fixed receiver units are installed around the field and regularly radio the transmitters worn by the players. When the sent signal strikes a transponder, it immediately emits electromagnetic waves (in the eponymous frequency range of micro and radar waves).

These waves disseminate consistently, but meet the recipients at differing points in time depending on their positions. Subsequently a central server calculates the exact position via triangulation from the information and sends the data to the analyst's laptop with minimal delay.

Therefore, the system delivers the data in real time, and furthermore "it benefits from the high accuracy and from being usable indoors." However, an elaborate installation is required at the stadium or training ground. This involves not only mounting the receivers on pylons or the like, but also a thorough calibration is needed to capture positions as accurately as possible. While not posing a major problem for the domestic training ground, this system is more complicated for away games or training camp. Furthermore, it needs to be considered that "the application is just possible in training because players are not yet permitted to wear transponders in competition," as Baca adds.

The problem with the prohibition of wearing of technical tools by players in competitions is a restriction that microwave-based systems share with GPS trackers. However, this may change soon as we will see in the following chapter. Until then, it should be noted that Messi features on the analyst's laptop in different ways. Which is best is to be judged on a case-by-case basis, because all systems come with advantages and disadvantages.

Depending on whether the data are collected in training or during a game, whether physical or tactical performance monitoring is the aim, or which financial framework is in place for the club, the choice can differ. One aspect must not be forgotten though, according to Baca: "It is essential that the used system is able to capture the ball position reliably as well." It does not work without the playing device.

INTERVIEW WITH GERMANY'S FIRST COMPUTER SPORTS SCIENTIST: PROF. DR. JÜRGEN PERL (CONTINUATION)

We have already talked with Jürgen Perl about the historical development of computer-based game analysis. We now look at progress in the area of hardware, for which he gave us insights into the technical side.

Have different techniques like stationary LPM, video systems, or GPS tracker been established? What are the differences among and problems of the acquisition technologies?

Different techniques become noticeable in the analysis especially due to the distinct quality of the data. Data errors caused by problems in acquisition have to be carefully corrected manually and/or require meticulous consistency in data analysis to avoid major mistakes.Meanwhile, however, automatically captured players' positional data of reasonable quality are available.

Is it also possible to accurately capture the ball position next to the players?

This still happens manually to a large extent and the data still show serious errors.

Are there currently still difficulties?

Yes, there are. The central error sources have already been discussed in detail at the workshop in Hochheim in 1989 and could not be corrected essentially by now. These include the clustering of players and the associated overlapping of player positions and the ball (camera systems) or overlays of inaccurate data (GPS tracker), which lead to breaks in the identification sequence and necessitate a new calibration respectively.

Which problems have not yet been solved satisfactorily?

On the one hand, the post-processing costs decline certainly with the number of cameras or with the accuracy of GPS trackers, but of course the investment costs increase and the comparability of the data, particularly of its precision, is not abundantly guaranteed in different installations any longer. On the other hand, especially for providers with two-camera-systems and associated complex manual follow-up, it is recommended to show restraint.

INTERVIEW WITH ERNST TANNER, RED BULL SALZBURG

The potential of accurate acquisition of positional data for a team, depends—as seen—on the favored application. Various possibilities exist, but there is no gold standard. Besides expert opinions from the academic sector, we will now have a look at the practical aspect.

For this purpose, we talked to Ernst Tanner, head of youth department of the Austrian league champions Red Bull Salzburg. He holds the UEFA-A license and worked as a coach of various youth teams for TSV 1860 Munich until 2009; from 2004 he was head of the youth academy. In 2009, he joined TSG 1899 Hoffenheim as head of the youth academy; in 2010 he became the athletics director and in 2011 managing director of sport. Since 2012 he has been head of the youth academy of FC Red Bull Salzburg. At one of the most advanced football academies in Europe, positional data are his daily companion at work. In the following interview, he provides an insight into his daily work routine and explains their choice of optimal tracking technology.

Dear Mr. Tanner, please give us an insight into the practical use of tracking technologies. With what kind of system do you work at youth level at RB Salzburg?

In Salzburg, we have a LPM system (Local Position Measurement) on three outside pitches as well as on one inside field. That is a radio-based system which can be used to track the player's position on the field as well as all movements with high precision. In addition, we are equipped with an optical ball tracking system on two of the outside pitches and on the inside field.

When and for what purpose are they used?

They are mainly used for the older academy teams U16 and U18, both in practice and home games. In practice mainly the athletic data are used for training control. The ball data from the games provide the basis for the technical-tactical match analysis.

How do you rate the different techniques on the market? What drives your ultimate choice of system?

First of all, it always depends on the purpose for which a system should be used for. If you only want to collect running data in the sense of a physical performance test or for training control, GPS-based systems appear to be sufficient, especially, since they are less expensive than other systems. However, the question about the validity of the data arises, specifically in regard to acceleration data. From our experience, these can only be inadequately determined.

In this sense, radio-based systems have a clear benefit. However, these are much more expensive and mostly stationary installed or the mobile variant is a little complex to set up. This becomes a problem when you have to travel a lot. The same is applicable for optical tracking systems. In addition to the effort required for the installation, appropriate time or financial capacity for the post-processing of the datasets is needed.

That means there is no universal solution?

If you want to capture the athletic data of the players from the training sessions, but also the ball data in order to gain technical-tactical knowledge from the games, you still have to rely on the combination of radio-based and optical systems. Therefore, there aren't any universal solutions, everyone has to find their individual solution, depending on the knowledge they want to gain from it.

4

COLLECTING DATA IN THE BUNDESLIGA

Game changer IFAB decision

As we have seen, there are many ways to generate positional data. However, the techniques that do not require camera systems have so far had the disadvantage that their use in competitive games is not permitted. These FIFA (International Federation of Association Football) rules include all systems consisting of electronic devices that the players have to carry around attached to their bodies. According to the statutes, these elements—which are not part of the standard clothing of a professional football player—are a taboo on the field.

But FIFA, or more precisely the International Football Association Board (IFAB), which is usually considered as somewhat conservative regarding technical innovation, has recently broken with this guideline. The committee, which consists of FIFA officials and representatives of the UK association, is the "guardian" of the official international football rules and has to approve any changes to these rules. At the IFAB's 129th annual meeting in Belfast at the beginning of 2015, it decided to allow the use of microchips in official games, in principle (see FIFA, 2015a).

However, the final decision on usage must be made by the national associations, which can individually decide whether and to what extent they want to allow the use of the new technologies. Only two conditions must be met, IFAB insists in a letter to FIFA members (see FIFA, 2015b): First, it has to be guaranteed that the devices used do not endanger the wellbeing of the players on the field—since their purpose is obviously the exact opposite. Before a team which is using the new technology is allowed to step onto the field, the refereeing team has to thoroughly check the devices and approve their use only when risks of any kind can be excluded.

The second limitation of use is related to the data collected. These may only be used for internal purposes. Any transfer to third parties, in particular for commercial purposes, is prohibited. In addition, the control commission forbids the use of electronic devices in the technical zone around the bench. This general restriction also affects the new tracking devices and thereby limits one of the greatest benefits of the new technology. If one wants to integrate live data into active coaching during the match, performance analysis is to be done within the half-time break.

Nevertheless, IFAB has with its decision opened the doors to the stadiums of Europe for positional data—a clear sign of what expectation has emerged from their Zurich headquarters. Looking at recent developments, this is a logical step, if not one that was long overdue. The possibilities that the 21st century offers are highly exciting for the game of football and worth more than just consideration. This is also reflected in the discussions about goal line technology and video assistant referees. While the former has already entered day-to-day league business, discussion about the latter is more recent. The first test phases have already taken place.

Yet football has perceived these latest achievements only as the latest chapter of many reforms that have taken place over the years. Especially rule changes have affected the game many times to become what we nowadays understand by modern football. There is for example the introduction of the offside rule or the change in the points system, which gave the winning team three instead of two points starting from season 1995–1996 (in national leagues).

It's no surprise that changes in rules are eyed critically. While the three point rule has now become a matter of fact, 66 per cent of national league professionals voted against the new rule when it was introduced by Leverkusen's former coach Erich Ribbeck calling it "nonsense" (see Nedo, 2015). Discussions about rule changes even date back to the transcription of the first set of rules itself. When the English Football Association met to finalize these, one particular point was heatedly discussed. Back then, the focus of the debate was the so-called "hacking," the deliberate kicking of the opponent's shin. The supporters of this, let's say tactical, ploy were ultimately unable to prevail (Wilson, 2008).

THE STATUS QUO OF THE BUNDESLIGA: INTERVIEW WITH HEAD OF TECHNOLOGY AND INNOVATION DFL, DR. HENDRIK WEBER

Following the decisions by IFAB, it seems we can look forward to GPS- or radar-based trackers in the national leagues. But on closer look, elaborate tracking systems are already being used in the European top leagues, including the 1st and 2nd Bundesliga in Germany. The German Football League (DFL) already had these systems installed in the 2013–2014 season and has been collecting data from all first and second league clubs ever since. In one aspect, the situation in the German national league is exceptional in Europe, as the DFL puts emphasis on equal access to the new information for all 36 clubs. It raises and distributes this centrally, and thus each club can not only analyze the performance of its own team, but also has full access to the data of other clubs, although how these data are analyzed needs to be decided by every club individually.

Besides the existing technologies, the DFL now has to consider how they can integrate wearable tracking systems into the German leagues. According to the fundamental decision by IFAB, it is their job to find a reasonable rule for the national competitions. Hence, we spoke to Dr. Hendrik Weber, from the DFL who is substantially involved in decision making. He combines the function of Head of Technology and Innovation with the DFL German Football League Ltd. and is thus also fully responsible for match analyses, data generation, and data marketing.

Dr. Weber remains CEO of the DFL Association SporTec Solutions Ltd., which among others is leading one of the most extensive live data promotions in football worldwide. He is also member of the FIFA expert group Electronic Performance and Tracking Systems, as well as initiator of the working group Match Analysis of the 36 professional clubs in the 1st and 2nd national leagues. Furthermore, he is co-author of many scientific publications and studies in the area of sport informatics as well as being a member of the advisory board of the master program Match Analysis at German Sports University Cologne.

Dear Dr. Weber, regarding the usage of wearable measuring equipment such as GPS units, the advisory board IFAB has transferred the responsibility to the respective leagues and clubs. These have to decide now about appropriate regulations. What about the German leagues?

After FIFA's decision in the 2015–2016 season, it was decided that so-called wearables should not yet be used during official matches, as according to the view of the DFL too many questions remained unanswered. Instead, a club task board was initiated: a group of experts with which meetings were held and aspects were discussed—among others, practical and legal questions. Afterwards we've come to the conclusion that "electronic performance and capturing systems (ELAS)," should be allowed starting the 2016–2017 season.

With "we" I mean the executive league board, who has released the decision as subsidiary committee and who is in charge of the license regulations. If the clubs want to use ELAS for their own means, they can now apply for the utilization at the DFL. If the DFL subsequently allows the respective equipment, the clubs can then use it in all competitions regulated by us.

What were the reasons behind the DFL's decision? What do those responsible hope to get from the authorization and use of this equipment?

The decision was supported by the DFL's open mindedness regarding innovations. Principally the DFL believes in the use of technologies in sport and especially in football and thus strongly supports them. In the end it is the club and not us who decides whether it wants to use the tools or not. And according to my current knowledge, the clubs are very interested in these possibilities. For example, to monitor players during their first matches after a longer injury break, to allow them the best re-integration to the match without getting injured again. To my knowledge this is currently the main goal of the clubs. Of course it would be great if a technical-tactical component was added. But actually the use was triggered from the athletic area.

In which context may a team use the equipment?

With its release, the clubs are allowed to use ELAS for all DFL games—of course limited to the internal match analysis including performance analysis. This means that neither commercial nor promotional use, nor the use of live data within the technical zone is allowed. There are different producers and the clubs are free to decide whichever they prefer.

The respective suppliers can indeed deliver different vital data. Thus, some may include measurements on heart frequency and others not. Some carry out many different measurements, but the clubs choose according to their needs and as long as the use remains internal, everything is fine. This means: At first the equipment is not limited regarding its sensors—as soon as a club has decided on a machine and it has been released, this is allowed and we thus approve it.

What does this approval depend on in praxis?

One criterion of the release is the players' and referees' danger of becoming injured by the chips. If they don't pose any danger—and if the use is also technically and technologically feasible—it is fine.

You said that the data may not the used live in the technical zone, meaning "online" . . .

Yes, checking the data online is forbidden. But this is a regulation by the FIFA and not by the DFL. As a club representative I could definitely say that this regulation does not make any sense. For example, it is forbidden to send information about the correctness of referee decisions to the bench after having looked at them externally. But this rule needs to be thought through.

This is the next logical step if this technology should be used. For the information is sent to the bank anyways, via text message or Smartwatch. Even if this is not officially allowed. The reason behind this limitation of the FIFA is their fear that a technical or mobile device is used at the sideline and thus the referee is not able to distinguish between moving image and data on the iPad. Thanks to video referee this regulation will be dropped someday.

In Germany the data are centrally collected and distributed. What about outside of the German league, is there collaboration between the top European leagues?

Spain and England are looking at the Bundesliga with envy, because there is no club-sharing internationally. Even a pan-European regulation will still take a while, as this is also a matter of rights and every competition is regulated nationally. And in other countries one can notice that solidarity stops at the border of the club. Luckily, in Germany this is not the case. Here, one can see the benefits of data exchange, from which everybody benefits. All in all, the entire league is improved.

Can the regulations in Germany serve as example for other European leagues? Could scouting for example benefit from international data exchange?

To put this thought one level higher and to say that this model would be good for all leagues is currently not feasible. Due to different sensitivities this scenario is still far away. English clubs for example don't want to be spied on in Champions League fixtures—whether they are playing against each other or against German teams.

Regarding scouting one can say that especially many companies would like to use these data. But the business models behind these ideas are rather business models that would take place outside of the clubs and leagues. Hence, we will not further look into this matter. Nevertheless it is recommendable for the UEFA to start to collect central tracking data for UEFA competitions, i.e., Champions League and Europa League, and to distribute them to all participants. This is currently not happening, but it would be a first step into the right direction.

References

FIFA (2015a). 129th Annual General Meeting of the International Football Association Board. Retrieved from: http://resources.fifa.com/mm/document/affederation/ifab/02/60/90/85/2015agm_minutes_v10_neutral.pdf

FIFA, 2015b. Approval of Electronic Performance and Tracking System (EPTS) Devices. Retrieved from: http://resources.fifa.com/mm/document/affederation/administration/02/66/27/59/circularno.1494-approvalofelectronicperformanceandtrackingsystem(epts)devices_neutral.pdf

Nedo, J. (2015). Vom Schwachsinn zum Standard. *Der Tagesspiegel*. Retrieved from: www.tagesspiegel.de/sport/20-jahre-drei-punkte-regel-vom-schwachsinn-zum-standard/12190850.html

Wilson, J. (2008). *Inverting the Pyramid: A History of Football Tactics*. Orion.

5

IN SEARCH OF THE HOLY GRAIL

Moneyball's heirs

In the age of Big Data, reports about data analyses in competitive sports are to be found everywhere. And it seems that in many sports currently the people responsible have acquired a taste for it. No surprise, as the more sophisticated a sport, the more difficult is the search for competitive advantages, the more creative and sometimes more unconventional become the approaches. When discussing this matter, there is often talk of "Moneyball"—a term quoted synonymously for the fairytale rise of the US-American baseball club, the Oakland Athletics, around the turn of the millennium.

For the financially not competitive A's, as they are commonly called in the US, every team's American dream came true: from the written off underdog to the celebrated champion. But it is not team spirit and commitment that play the main roles in the story around manager Billy Beane, it is the analytic considerations of the passionate baseball fan Bill James and his analyses that led the team from Oakland to their unexpected rise, turning Major League Baseball upside down by the way.

Of course revolutions are part of the development in sports and every kind of sport makes its own history. They can be of practical or tactical nature, induced by changes in rules "from above" or come along with the technological developments. In Moneyball there was a new aspect, which was previously mostly underestimated: systematic match analysis by means of bare numbers. Indeed, statistics had already been involved in decision making in sports by that time. But the models developed by James were simply better—and raised the genre to a completely new level.

The seminal approach resulted in key advantages on the transfer market, and with their methods the Athletics managed to sign highly underestimated players inexpensively and to equate the financial disadvantage to baseball heavyweights like the Yankees or Red Sox. Between 2000 and 2003 they reached the playoffs three times in succession and achieved an unmatched series of wins with 20 unbeaten games, a feat unequalled to this day and a success which no expert had ever predicted.

The story sounds more like Hollywood than a true incident, since next to a sports success story it also provides hero and anti-hero at the same time, in the shape of the innovative manager Beane and the likeable number cruncher, James. By this, it is hardly surprising that after the eponymous literary realization by Michael Lewis (Lewis, 2004), the watchable film *Moneyball* appeared on the screens. Today, "Moneyball" enjoys recognition not only among baseball spectators. Fans of all kinds of sports have absorbed the success story and have begun to search for their own Bill James ever since.

Quite literally, by looking at the statements of Gavin Fleig, head of the analysis department of the English football club Manchester City. He provided, free of charge, the proprietary dataset of a full Premier League season in 2012 in cooperation with the data company Opta. "Bill James kick-started the analytics revolution in baseball. That made a real difference and has become integrated in that sport. Somewhere in the world there is football's Bill James, who has all the skills and wants to use them but hasn't got the data. We want to help find that Bill James, not necessarily for Manchester City but for the benefit of analytics in football" is how he justified the publishing of the usually strict confidential information (Hunter, 2012).

The short-term success of Fleig's attempt remains negligble, but it shows with which expectations people working at an elite level face the increasing flood of data. Whether basketball, golf, American football, or football—the search for the winning formula runs at full speed in almost every kind of sport. That baseball has set this ball rolling is by no means an accident however, but is largely dependent on the comparably readily analyzable nature of the game. Although it is a team sport, baseball can be broken down into chunks of play and individual perform- ances, an enormously effective strategy. Furthermore, component time plays virtually no role as actions on the field follow one another linearly.

What works well in baseball cannot hence automatically be transferred to other team sports in practice. Sports games like football, basketball, or hockey are far more dynamic, the transitions are fluent, and many players interact in a highly complex fashion and form a non-linear course of action. In short, what happens on the pitch can't be expressed in numbers in as straightforward a manner as in baseball. In football, the circumstance that after 90 minutes occasionally just a single goal may make the difference between defeat and victory is just another obstacle.

Yet, with the introduction of positional data completely new possibilities have opened up in a whole range of sports. Before we focus exclusively on football again in the remainder of this book, we now want to step outside the box. Whether team or individual sports, positional data can be found in many of these around the globe. And in some, revolutions as in "Moneyball" have just started.

The list is long, including American football, basketball, hockey, tennis, beach volleyball, athletics, and even motorsports and ice speed skating. Just as experienced football coaches find new impetus in training theory and match tactics of other sports every so often, we will now see current developments in some of these. We start, of course, with baseball.

Baseball: The data freaks' experimental laboratory

With the Athletics' achievements during the "Moneyball" years, a new era in baseball statistics began. Nowadays, producing and evaluating analyses for player assessment is not only a popular hobby among a huge fan community, but is also firmly established in the top club's front offices. And by now also in the language. The portmanteau Sabermetrics, composed of the abbreviation SABR (Society for American Baseball Research) and the word metrics, has established and synonymously stands for the number-based perspective of baseball.

Sabermetrics is so popular that technical innovations are downright longed for by the fans. Skepticism towards innovations is not noticeable in the technically affine America, and especially for fans of the Yankees, Red Sox, and Co. the desire for something new is predominant. Thus, for example the system PITCHf/x developed by the company Sportvision, and applied for the first time in 2006, enjoyed great popularity. While the system was in use, two cameras recorded every pitch and dissected it in detail. For instance, throwing velocity, the trajectory, and the exact place where the ball reaches the home base, at which the batter waits for the ball. Whether the curve-, fast-, or knuckleball, the latter known in football as well from Cristiano Ronaldo's infamous free kicks, with the new technique the spectators were able to follow even the most uncommon trajectories straight to the point.

But what's more, nine seasons later PITCHf/x had already been replaced Statcast. After a trial season, Statcast is now installed in all Major League Baseball ballparks and opens up a whole new range of possibilities. The system combines video tracking, as it is also applied in football, with a radar-based tracking system. Because there are no microchips set into the ball, however, the technology takes advantage of the Doppler effect known from physics to localize the ball on the pitch.

The same technique is also deployed in golf, where nowadays hardly any professional refrains from accurately testing his shots. In baseball, both techniques are laid on top of each other and are aligned in real time. With 32 frames per second, during an ordinary baseball game about seven terabytes of data are accumulated. Therefore, not even one half of a game can be accommodated on the hard drive of an ordinary laptop. But the data are abundant with information, since next to the combined tracking technology also a number of new metrics belong to Statcast, which might take away all baseball fans' breath.

It starts with the so-called *pitch*. Here information about throwing velocity or rotation speed (number of cycles per second) is readily available for both spectators and analysts. If the batter standing at the *home base* strikes the ball, the moment of *batting*, the KPI machinery really gets going. When leaving the bat, the velocity and launch angle of the ball are measured. The exact trajectory of the ball can be recorded in the air, including information on flight duration and width, and—in case of a *homerun*, the successful strike of the ball beyond the outfield—even the projected flight duration and width. The spectator then sees how far the ball would have flown if the stadium was not limited physically by the stands.

If the ball is in the air, batter and teammates already standing at the *bases* try to cover as many of them as possible. For these runs, for example, acceleration and maximum speed are measured from the pathways captured. At the same time, the defending team tries to catch the batted ball in the outfield, preferably in the air of course, and to throw back to the bases in order to eliminate the runners. Here as well, data concerning acceleration and velocity are available, as well as the velocity of the balls thrown back.

Pioneering this technological revolution are two new performance indicators that can be used against the criticized lack of defensive metrics. First, the catcher's reaction speed, assessed to the point in time when he starts moving after a successful bat, and his so-called running efficiency. The latter is recorded as percentage value and rates the congruence of a catcher's pathway and the ideal route between his starting position and landing position of the ball. Statcast makes a little secret of how the exact figure is calculated in the end, but the catchers' animated pathways are already providing intriguing insights into the accuracy with which an *outfielder* can predict the trajectory of a ball.

Especially these defensive statistics have been used intensively by clubs for performance analysis since the introduction of tracking data. This is most obvious in the number of so-called *defensive shifts*, which have doubled almost every season since 2011 (Helfand, 2015). During a *defensive shift*, the defenders do not line up in the traditional formation in which they would be evenly distributed around the bases, but push to one direction depending on the adversarial batter's batting profile.

If the data show for example that the batter predominantly strikes the ball to the right side of the field, it might also happen that the defenders all move to one side. Exactly this profile is shown for example by the most valuable player (MVP) of the 2013 World Series and recently retired superstar, David Ortiz. when he was ready to bat at the home base in his last season as an active player, almost all defenders moved to the right side of the field.

INTERVIEW WITH CHUCK KORB, SABERMETRICS GURU AND ANALYST OF THE BOSTON BRUINS

In respect of data analysis, baseball is still the measure of all things. The enthusiasm for numbers and statistics is not entirely on the part of the fans, but is an important topic in the managers' offices as well. To gain a better insight, we spoke with Chuck Korb.

He has worked with the Boston Bruins in a senior analytics position for the past 2+ seasons.

Chuck's first love is baseball, however, and he is the founder of the annual Sabermetrics, Scouting, and the Science of Baseball seminar (www.saber seminar.com), whose proceeds are used for the charitable purposes of the Jimmy Fund and the Angioma Alliance. When he is not running numbers, Chuck can be found at Fenway Park, or surfing on Good Harbor Beach. In the interview, he revealed how Statcast could lift baseball to a new level—and that in respect of positional data the NHL lags behind other kinds of sport.

Dear Mr. Korb, Statcast is the newest toy for the data-loving baseball fan. Besides great entertainment, what is the benefit for the clubs and their analysis departments?

I think there is value to Statcast, but it will take a lot of data to get there. For example, when assessing a player's defensive value it would be great to know how far an "average" outfielder can travel on a ball hit at x MPH and a y angle. Knowing the average first step, maximum speed, average speed, and route efficiency of every player on every ball hit could lead to an extremely accurate defensive evaluation system. Pitching assessment also has great potential with Statcast. Knowing the location, velocity, movement, spin rate, etc., of each different type of pitch could both allow greater evaluation of pitcher skills, as well as give the manager a way to watch for issues—i.e., velocity down, arm angle different, etc., which could help with injury prevention. Batting is similar. Knowing the speed of the ball off the bat, the angle it's hit, backspin or topspin, etc., with enough data could allow someone to estimate how well a batter "should" perform based on their batted balls. Because this eliminates luck (bloop hits, line drives into gloves, etc.) it should stabilize faster and allow estimations of future performance on a smaller sample.

Has Sabermetrics now fully infiltrated every aspect of baseball? Where does this fascination for data come from?

Sabermetrics is absolutely in every aspect of baseball, as it should be. The goal is to win games, and teams use any information available to help them do so. Using analytics, science, film study, etc., and traditional scouting are cost effective ways to add the extra little bit that can get a team over the top. The talent cost of a win in baseball is somewhere around $8,000,000. If you can gain even a portion of a win from finding an undervalued asset, or a skill other teams may not be considering like pitch framing, it can be a great benefit to the team. Jonah Keri wrote a great book about the Tampa Bay Rays, The Extra 2 per cent, and that's what Sabermetrics is trying to do, add that extra 2 per cent. I also want to make it clear that teams have not and should not abandon traditional scouting/observation when assessing players and teams.

The most effective (and in my opinion the best) teams use a combination of sabermetrics/statistics, science, and scouting.

Generally speaking, baseball seems to be a spearhead in terms of data analytics in sport. How far on this route is hockey, particularly in terms of positional data?

Hockey analytics are in their infancy; we are just starting to try to figure out what "works" and what doesn't. Hockey is very different than baseball, and much more difficult to assess statistically. That is not to say it cannot be done, but while baseball is a static sport which lends itself to Markovian and linear weights analyses, hockey is a flowing event with players changing rapidly and often. We are progressing in hockey analytics, and it is very exciting being in on the initial stages, but hockey is light years behind baseball right now. Hockey does not have a good handle on positional data—the NHL has not yet placed cameras in each venue, so there is no universal player tracking. When that comes, and some teams are already doing it on their own, it will be a huge step.

How do the other major US sports compare?

I think basketball is the closest major U.S. sport to baseball in terms of analytics. They have had a revolution in the NBA, with teams hiring analytic staffs, doing advanced player tracking—the NBA does have cameras in each stadium for this purpose—and with many coaches buying into the use of stats and video/science. An aside here, one of the biggest roadblocks to teams instituting, or attempting to institute, the use of advanced statistics in player acquisition and team strategy is the willingness of the coaching staff and/or front office to accept and listen to the data. The NHL is probably next is the use of analytics among the 4 major U.S. sports, and I've spoken about them at some length above. The NFL is just starting to embrace analytics, but it will grow exponentially very quickly, much as it has in other sports.

Now this is a tough one: What can football learn from baseball and vice versa?

After watching some of the football presentations at the Sports Analytics conference in Manchester, what struck me most was how far football is ahead of all US major sports in their use of science and analytics in player training. Taking a scientific individual player approach to which muscles to overload, when to push and when to rest, what to eat, how much to sleep, etc., using biometric machines, fitness trackers, wearable technology, etc., gives the team and players a huge advantage, and is something missing in the U.S.

Football, like hockey, is a flowing sport, and not as easy to assess as baseball. Where they can learn from baseball, however, is in the use of laser technology and high speed cameras, like StatCast, to find players' first step speed, maximum velocity, how optimally the run to the ball, etc. Also, in general, baseball teaches all sports that there are benefits to be gained from the use of analytics, and to keep looking for a way to find that extra 2 per cent!

Hockey: Know-how for the national teams

In contrast to baseball, hockey is distinctly more similar to football. And distinctly further regarding data-based match analysis in comparison to the related sport of ice hockey. For football these developments are particularly interesting because both kinds of sport resemble each other on a basic level quite a bit. Especially field hockey shows major congruities in matters of number of players, object of the game, field size, and tactical elements.

Hockey can and will therefore always give a worthwhile comparison. It is not without good reason that several experts switch fields between the two disciplines from time to time. As did the former German hockey national coach Bernhard Peters and recently also Markus Weise. In 2015, after having won three Olympic gold medals the latter became coach of the German women's and also the men's team from the DHB to the DFB, where he is helping to create the contentual setup of the new DFB academy, a national intensive training center of German football, as a concept developer.

INTERVIEW WITH ULRICH FORSTNER, NATIONAL COACH "SCIENCE AND EDUCATION"

The expertise in hockey is also desired in football. It remains to be seen to what extent data-based match analysis is involved. However, the current situation is highly promising. Especially the German hockey federation is very open with respect to innovations in match analysis, and new developments are always supported. We talked to Ulrich Forstner, youth national coach of the DHB, to find out how this looks works in detail.

Ulrich Forstner has been full-time national coach "science and education" of the German Hockey Federation since 2010. After studying Sports and Physics (to become a teacher) at the Albert-Ludwigs-University in Freiburg and Sports (Diploma) at University Basel, he was hired for a full-time position as a state hockey coach by the state sports federation Baden-Württemberg. Then, he took over the U16 and U18 teams as head coach. As the full-time national coach of the German Hockey Federation for the male youth department/U21 coach, he achieved numerous podium positions in 2009 (World Cup 2001: 3rd place, Euro Cup 2002: 2nd place, Euro Cup 2004: 2nd place, Euro Cup 2006: 2nd place, Euro Cup 2008: 3rd place, World Cup 2009: 1st place).

Dear Mr. Forstner, can you give us an insight into how match analysis in hockey started to take positional data into account?

At the beginning, the focus was on tracking the distances run by the players as well as their running speeds and their development over the whole course of a match. On the one hand, to be able to draw conclusions on existing performance control and, on the other hand, on individual stress profiles for the different positions. These statements were quickly judged to be superficial, and that is why we tried to find ways to map individual fatigue among players through positional data.

What happened afterwards?

We were then occupied with the recording of reliable acceleration values and thus with the accuracy and reliability of the systems. Parallel to this collection we also recorded positional data via GPS systems during international games, which should be concerned about quantitative aspects—how many passes, how many ball losses?—And also tactical questions with the help of the well-known video analysis method: from which player does my attacker receive his/her passes? Directly from the defense or rather from the midfield? Which ones lead to goal chances or to penalty corners—and which do not? And so on . . .

Qualitative or quantitative analysis, which metrics have proven to be helpful in hockey?

The most often used performance indicators are goals, goal chances, penalty corners, entering the shooting circle and into the attack quarter, passes, dribbling, long corners, free hits, ball gains, and ball losses. Generally, it is all about pure counting of match actions. The performance indicators are also presented in the form of relations, as they are more suitable than counting, to assess the game effectiveness of the team. Furthermore, these actions are analyzed in sequences, to display game patterns.

This sounds promising. Are these new approaches in game analysis also used in practice?

We use many different methods in national and international matches and in training measurements.

So one can actually detect the influence of the data?

Of course one can feel the influence of Big Data. The data volume is constantly growing and it always needs to be questioned, which utility and significance they finally have for the athlete and/or the coach. And the relation between effort and utility needs to be scrutinized and perhaps limited.

Which developments do you expect in the future? How will new technologies in data analysis change sports?

Looking into the future I can see the following developments: positional data recordings will become easier, less complicated and more precise. Hence, further interesting areas will evolve.

For example?

Determining a fatigue coefficient live during the game or training for example. Or individual energy levels with consequences for hydration and nutrition during training and competition.

Which other developments can you see?

Quantitative recordings, i.e., positional data, have to be combined even more with qualitative aspects like video analysis or expert opinions to become more informative. Then relevant consequences for training and competition control as well as for coaching can be deducted. One big quality step in hockey would be the possibility to also capture positional data for the ball.

Beach volleyball: Analyses at the Copacabana

More and more data are collected in beach volleyball, a sport which is becoming ever more popular—even during the Olympic Games in Rio 2016, as the sport scientist Dr. Daniel Link explains. He is a computer scientist in sports at the Institute for Training Sciences and Sport Informatics at TU Munich and, together with national league coach Jörg Ahmann, he has developed a match analysis procedure for beach volleyball based on positional data. The respective software tools are setting the standard in match observation in the German Volleyball Association today, and were a crucial component of the preparation that led to the German teams winning gold medals in London 2012 and Rio de Janeiro 2016.

In the interview he furthermore describes that the tactical area is currently still rated distinctly higher than that concerning physical performance. This is a bit surprising if one considers that players specifically try to fatigue exhausted opponents by preferably passing the ball to them. On the other hand, substitutions as we know them from football are not possible in beach volleyball—the one who cannot play on has to pass. Nevertheless, Link sees a benefit for the load control in training.

Yet, the comparison to football is still exciting because in football physical analysis currently still predominates in practice, at least in terms of positional data. Yet, analysts could by all means draw some inspiration from their colleagues in the sand who search for patterns in the teams' moves with the help of the newly available data. By categorizing rallies in their courses systematically, certain offensive schemata can be filtered out.

Now, in regard of tactical considerations, beach volleyball has some advantage over football since offense and defense are separated much more clearly. In addition to that comes the subtle difference that the analyst has to deal with only two instead of eleven players. Nonetheless, what works on the small scale could as well be transferred to the large scale. Indeed, the analysts involved in beach volleyball showed how it could work in football only to a small extent—but they are certainly a role model.

This is because Link and his team are quite successful with their approach. They have managed to combine data-based analysis efficiently with conventional video analysis. The data supply them with a preselection of scenes of play which can subsequently be evaluated manually. At the Olympics this process worked out well: After the men's gold medal win in London 2012, Laura Ludwig and Kira Walkenhorst made it to the top of the podium in Rio de Janeiro four years later—an achievement which no European women's team has ever done before.

INTERVIEW WITH DR. DANIEL LINK, SPORTS SCIENTIST AT TU MUNICH

Dr. Link, how can beach volleyball be analyzed with positional data and where is beach volleyball in comparison to other kinds of sport?

To answer this question, it makes sense to distinguish between tactical and conditional performance diagnostics. In the field of conditional factors, positional data can certainly help to assess the athletes' energetic load. Optical tracking methods, as they are deployed in the professional area of football or US sports, have not been able to prevail so far for financial reasons.

So-called Electronic Performance and Tracking Systems (EPTS) based on GPS are an alternative. They are worn directly on the body and require quite little maintenance. There are indeed some case studies in this area, but I still do not know any team deploying these systems in their training routine. Beach volleyball is still at an early stage here.

And in the tactical area?

We are significantly further in tactical analyses. Since 2011, we have deployed positional data for the German national teams' match analysis. We use no temporal high-resolution movement trajectories but merely eight positions of the players at certain points in time, which we ascertain manually. This includes for example the receiving player's position at ball contact, the offensive and defensive position and the blocker's position at the offender's jump.

With these positions, the rallies are classified then, for example by the offensive player's run-up direction or the block's and defensive players' spatial configuration shortly prior to the attacking strike. From this, equivalence classes of play situations develop, providing the basis for the subsequent match analysis.

Which performance indicators or methods seem to be most suitable?

We use a three-stage method. In a first step equivalence classes of match situations are formed as described. Within these equivalence classes, the opponent's behavior is described in the second step. For offensive actions in volleyball, this is the information if a hard strike or a *shot*, meaning a high strike over the block with an arched trajectory, is performed, to which sector of the field the ball heads and how successful the action was. Performance indicators for the defense are the block direction and the blocker's arm position as well as the defending player's running behavior. This information is partially derived from the positional data.

How do you use this information?

We assume that even top-class athletes have conscious or subconscious action tendencies in similar situations, especially in pressure situations. We try to find these with the values of the performance indicators in the equivalence classes. It is important for me to point out that the quantification over performance indicators is just an intermediate step. We never rely on numbers, but use these only for generating hypotheses, which are examined then in the third step, the qualitative analysis of the video footage. To run the entire process efficiently, we have developed two analytics tools with longstanding support of Federal Institute for Sport Science (BISp), the BeachScouter for the collection of data and the BeachViewer for the analysis.

Where and how are the new methods of game analysis deployed in practice? Is there already a noticeable influence of Big Data?

The tools have been deployed routinely in the top-class area in Germany since 2011. A match analyst supports the top athletes and their coaches in almost every tournament of the FIVB World Tour. Currently this is Ron Gödde and Raimund Wenning from the Olympic center Stuttgart, who do an outstanding job here. They make video recordings of the opponents, code several basic characteristics of the rallies and capture the positional data. Then this package is provided for the teams over a central database. In the junior sector this process happens as well, but not that extensive. In the end, it is a question of resources.

Are there already examples of the success of this approach?

The OSP Stuttgart alone has evaluated a total of 310 international games in the first half year 2016 in preparation for the Olympic Games in Rio de Janeiro —64 more during the tournament (see Figure 5.1). This database served as a starting point for the German teams' strategy development.

We could really notice other nations' interest in our approach at the Copacabana—which we did not serve of course. I think it is fair to say that Big Data contributed its part to the Olympic victories of Ludwig/Walkenhorst in Rio, but as well to the victory of Brink/Reckermann in London 2012.

Which developments are you expecting next? How will new data analysis technologies change the sport?

I assume that EPTS will gain in importance. These devices become ever smaller and can be worn on the body without considerable interferences.I see the use for training control in the first place because the training load can be quantified very well by that and the athletes' course of exhaustion can be assessed individually. For instance, it is interesting in beach volleyball, whether and if so, in which situations the maximum jump altitude is not realized or when performance-affecting losses of jumping power arise.

FIGURE 5.1 Game analysis at the Copacabana during the Rio 2016 Olympics

Probably the development in the top-class area will take a similar course like in professional football—although attenuated because the financial possibilities are different. We are conducting first pilot studies at the moment in cooperation with national coach Jörg Ahmann and his squad athletes for the application of EPTS in beach volleyball. He is very open-minded towards technological innovations and internationally one of the leading minds concerning the development of beach volleyball.

Tennis: from Hawk-Eye to player profiles

Also in racket sports positional data have complemented conventional video analysis in recent years. Thus for example in tennis, where the Hawk-Eye system has supported the referees in their decisions as to whether a ball has hit the ground inside or outside the court for more than a decade. However, the application of the tracking technologies is currently beyond the scope of the application as a referees' technical aid.

Those who watch the major Grand Slam tournaments consistently will know the vivid visualizations of where the players direct their serves and returns to. And in both the professionals' and several amateurs' training routines the PlaySight system, which records the game with six fixed cameras and locates actions on the field similar to the Hawk-Eye technology, is enjoying increasing popularity.

In practice, most professionals still refer to their coaches' subjective decisions. However, objective information will make it possible to examine these in the future. Then it can be checked by means of bigger datasets, e.g., which strike can be most successful in certain situations and against which players. Basically, it is now theoretically possible to precisely detect tennis professionals' strong and weak points.

This must be neither a disadvantage nor a suspense killer, as some people argue because ultimately, the same data are available for all top-class players. Prospectively it will rather depend on how the information is applied for preparation and during a match. Who will manage to take maximum advantage of the opponent's player profile and to surprise their opponent simultaneously—the opponent knows his/her own profile, too, of course—by changing one's own patterns? These new data could lift the sport tactically to a whole new level.

INTERVIEW WITH TENNIS PROFESSIONAL DOMINIK MEFFERT

Currently, these considerations are dreams of the future. But what is the state of play? In the following interview, Dominik Meffert, former top-200 player, reveals how positional data are about to become established in tennis. Since 2015 he has been teaching special tasks with a focus on tennis at the

German Sport University in Cologne. During his playing career, he took part in all four Grand Slam tournaments and achieved four singles and fifteen doubles victories against ATP challengers. He was five times German champion with TK Kurhaus Lambertz Aachen, twice French champion with AS Patton Rennes, and Swiss champion once with TC Wollerau.

Dear Mr. Meffert, what is the current state of the art in tennis?

In comparison to other kinds of sport, tennis is still in the development stage, in practice it has not been worked with analysis that strongly. The good players have their coaches who attend games of the next opponent, watch them and take notes. But with certainty there will be programs in which information on where a certain player serves or his favorite moves are listed. This simply makes sense and it would be disastrous if it would not develop to that.

Are there first signs for this development already?

There are, and it is getting more and more. PlaySight for example is doing a lot and so does IBM as well at the Grand Slam tournaments. And there will still happen a whole lot more. The latest system is PlaySight, recommended by the DTB and installed in Chorweiler at Tennis Mittelrhein. This is great because PlaySight provides all the data and the players' movements as well as the strikes can be seen.

Furthermore, the players can be looked at from all possible angles. First and foremost, PlaySight serves facts and thus, tasks of the player can be checked instantly. Errors can be viewed, it is possible to rewind and to precisely analyze strikes. The system is very good and will shortly be installed almost everywhere at the regional training centers. That is the first step in the right direction.

You talked about movements and strikes: How can tennis be analyzed in practice?

Strike direction and the players' positions are the two main criteria for the analysis of tennis. It is captured where the ball is hit to and how the players move in the back. This can be seen in these clouds on TV. Take for example Angelique Kerber, she always stands a little bit further behind the line than Serena Williams. In the men's competitions Novak Djokovic always stands right on the baseline when playing a return. Other players have a different position and of course it is interesting to see, which position brings which success. Not only how the players do it, but also what results from this. Are they successful with their positioning or are they not? By this, wrong decisions can be reconsidered for the next game.

Rafael Nadal, for instance, has deviated from his pattern in the last match in which he was able to beat Djokovic. Usually, he always plays 60–70 or even 80 per cent of his serves against his opponent's backhand. But Djokovic's backhand is the best return worldwide. At that time, when he beat him in this match in Monte Carlo, he completely deviated from his pattern and played 80 per cent of his serves against the forehand. That means, he has reflected on himself before the match: What have I done wrong and what am I going to do different this time?

Finally, a brief look at the future. Where is this journey going?

These techniques are used more and more. People realize that it is important and how big the influence of big data on tennis is. At some point, it will be standard that the player has a small booklet or something similar in which it is noted how certain players have played before. This is going to happen, just like in football. Obviously, there is still going to be the surprise effect. But if you know what your opponent's favorite ball usually is, you can adapt to the opponent and improve your own performance. This can serve as the basis for calculations.

References

Helfand, Z. (July 19, 2015). Use of defensive shifts in baseball is spreading—because it works. *Los Angeles Times*. Retrieved from: www.latimes.com/sports/la-sp-baseball-defensive-shifts-20150719-story.html

Hunter, A. (August 16, 2012). Manchester City to open the archive on player data and statistics. *The Guardian*. Retrieved from: www.theguardian.com/football/blog/2012/aug/16/manchester-city-player-statistics

Keri, J. (2011). *The extra 2%: How Wall Street strategies took a major league baseball team from worst to first*. New York: ESPN Books/Ballantine Books.

Lewis, M. (2004). *Moneyball: The art of winning an unfair game*. New York: WW Norton.

6

BETTING AND SPORTS ANALYTICS

A remarkable approach

Let's imagine a football club that—despite all concerns—does not mind risks and puts data into the focus of its work. A club that not only trusts the expertise of its scouts when acquiring players for millions, but a club that also tries to objectify its decisions with the help of elaborate analyses. A club that constantly invents new tactical tricks based on event and positional data, to surprise their opponents. Could something like that work? Or is football too complex to allow these crazy ideas to become reality?

Fortunately, we need not continue these thoughts to find an answer, as an example of a data-led football club already exists. It is situated in Herning, in the middle of Jutland, playing in the Danish Super League and is called FC Midtjylland. And this club is determined to leave nothing to chance. Their success? In 2015 the club celebrated the first championship win in its history and, in the following Europa League season, they managed to win at home against highly favored Manchester United.

All of this started with a crazy idea, followed by a combination of mathematical know-how and a bold approach. A project was born that is truly unequalled in European football. In the center of it all is Matthew Benham, a physicist and now owner of both FC Midtjylland and his beloved English club, FC Brentford. Benham's career began as derivative trader in London's financial district before dedicating his career to betting in football (Biermann, 2015). He started his own company, and through the use of ingenious mathematical models he was able to outperform the bookies.

Financial success was massive, enabling Benham to pursue his vision in the world of top league football. In the summer of 2012 he acquired the majority stake in FC Brentford, the club which he had supported since childhood. Two years later, FC Midtjylland followed. Both clubs have been ruled by the data ever since: in scouting, in match preparation and post-analyses, in training—actually everywhere.

Those in charge are not concerned that their approaches are too radical. Rather they question every single aspect of the daily work routine in a professional football club and try to optimize these with the help of mathematical models. They have invented a calculated ranking system of all European teams, for example, a kind of table of performance levels. International fixtures help the model to overcome the limits of national competitions. What remains is an international comparison of all teams, regardless of Premier League or 2nd Bundesliga, etc.

The results are not just pretty calculations, but for instance help to compensate for financial disadvantages in the transfer market. Before winning the league in season 2014–2015, the Wolves, as they are commonly called, signed Tim Sparv from SpVgg Greuther Fürth for a mere €300,000. Sparv was a solid second-league player, but not particularly known to have exceptional skills. Why bother to sign someone who appears to be only an average lower-league player? The answer is very simple: According to the model's calculations, Greuther Fürth could have played in the Premier League according to its performance in the previous season. And the Finish Sparv, being the player most often used, played a decisive supporting defensive role in midfield.

A club without ears or eyes

Even when it comes to tactics, the managing staff do not rely solely on their own eyes, but rather the numbers. The team, consisting of a psychiatry coach and a neurobiologist working with the coaches, is especially fond of standard situations. No other situation can bring such important results with such little effort. But the "Midtjylland Revolution," as the magazine *11Freunde* once called the project (Biermann, 2013), is more than smoke and mirrors. With the help of these new approaches, the club's very first championship win was secured and today the Wolves are among the Danish top tier. During the season they topped the table, averaging one goal per game and a standard situation on average—and Sparv showed what he could deliver.

What methods are utilized in Denmark is a well-kept secret. However, Benham's and his partner Rasmus Ankersen's vision for the future is no secret. In an interview with the Dutch journalist Michiel de Hoog (De Hoog, 2015), Ankersen revealed the trust they are putting in their own approach: "The position in the table within the own ranking is more important for performance evaluation than the actual placement in the Danish Super League. And the idea is not to send any scouts to matches for player recruitment any longer."

In any case, as they reason, one single game is not very significant. The experts should rather trust video recordings of many matches—and data. Ankersen's quote probably summarizes best what is currently happening in Denmark: "We redesigned the club based on a question: What would a football club look like if it had no human eye and ear? Of course, it turns out you need a human element. But if you say from the start that 'Oh, it has to be a combination of stats and humans,' then you won't be radical enough to be able to make a difference."

One needs to wait and see whether FC Midtiylland will have long-term success with its approach. Nevertheless, the club is playing an important role when it comes to integrating data into top-class sports, as there is no comparable experiment to be found anywhere else in Europe. A smaller league, like the Danish one, thereby serves as an ideal testing ground for this radical undertaking. But surely not everything will work out instantly for the Wolves? Some ideas—and the doers have a lot of them—will turn out to be unsuccessful, but that too is part of the game.

Pioneers such as Benham and Ankersen are extremely important for the development of these ideas. Thanks to their decisiveness and devotion to experimentation, it will not take long before we can marvel at crazy free kick routines and can look forward to further innovations from Denmark's experimental approach. Yet, club owner and initiator of the story, Benham is not fond of the comparison being made to Moneyball and Bill James—according to his statements in various interviews.

INTERVIEW WITH LARS CHRISTENSEN, FC MIDTJYLLAND

Recently, the Danish super league decided to have the positional data of all league fixtures recorded and Midtjylland is already working on this. We talked to Lars O.D. Christensen from FC Midtjylland about the influence this approach will have on day-to-day affairs at the club and about how much progress the Wolves are making.

Christensen did his master's thesis in Sports Science and Human Physiology and holds a Ph.D. in Neurophysiology. He did academic work at universities in Denmark and England and has taught at many levels in sports physiology and neurophysiology, biomechanics, cognitive neuroscience, and exercise and motor control. Since 2015 he has worked at FC Midtjylland, with a focus on talent development, exercise methods, data analysis, cognitive diagnostics, learning theory, perception of training, and the use of data in decision-making processes.

Dear Mr. Christensen, not only for fans of data analysis is FC Midtjylland one of the most interesting clubs in European football. After winning the Danish Super League in 2015, where is the project now?

Thank you on behalf of the club. The project has already taken many twists and turns during my period in the club (from January 2015)—including people out and new people in—but data analysis is more relevant than ever. After a period of undoubted success, culminating in the Danish Championship 2015, the main part of the coaching team has gradually been changed and we therefore had to expect a period of difficult transition. This happened together with a relatively successful season for us, especially in Europe League, which is very resource consuming. Time to develop and move the project forward was therefore limited, especially regarding the daily activities. We have learnt the lesson that major changes and this kind of development, do not go hand in hand with a very tight match schedule. But now we are back in full action on all parameters and we hope to setup more and still new approaches here. We are working in a number of new directions, including positional data in new ways and in a new setup. We find this very interesting and hope in addition, that we will be able to tie the coaching staff closer to the actual analysis, which I find is a key point at this time. Therefore, three points have been made clear for us, you need quite some time for the entire staff to implement strong data-analysis, you need the coaching staff involved at a basic level already and you need even more game-related data output, than done so far, which I think is most likely to come from the addition of positional data.

Data play a vital role in decision making at the club. How does that work in practice? Are there still areas where you proceed in "the traditional way"?

Many "ways" in the club are and always have been the traditional way, i.e., it has been imperative for us to have the coaches as closely involved in the process as possible and when we have drifted away from this, it has been corrected. In other words, it is important for the club to try as hard as possible to maintain a strong coherence between all parties participating in the work. In certain areas we may even return to the traditional "traditional ways" in the club, but I am not involved in any of this, so I will not comment further.

One key area is to be able to combine different types of knowledge, like data obtained technologically with data gained from human experience, in an optimal manner. This is difficult, but a key problem to fix, in order to advance the field as a whole. We are developing a number of different approaches to optimize this, which is ranging from educational tools to employing modern cognitive science and types of analyses and to focusing on (for us) new tactical concepts, etc., which are partly based on data and partly on coach-experiences in order to generate this coherence. We hope it works.

Briefly, in practice we use data at a number of levels as it is. They are central for the physical training, for game-evaluation, etc., for developing and implementing new tactical elements, for optimizing individual technical training, for player profiling—mental to physical—and for player evaluation, internally and externally.

The Danish Super League recently agreed with a major tracking data supplier to collect data throughout the league. How will the clubs benefit from that new source of information?

At the moment, we are not really involved in all of this, so I do not know how it will influence us eventually.

Will the new data stream be integrated in the data-driven approach by FC Midtjylland or has it been already? What would that look like?

We are already involved in integrating new types of data and analyses, which at least partly is strongly focused on the positional data. Bigger data including more teams and/or leagues will open up for new avenues in terms of research and analysis, which could be a catalyst for new ways of thinking in football. No more comments here.

In terms of future perspectives: What new insights about the game can positional data analysis offer in comparison to what currently available data can do? Where do you see the greatest potential?

Event-data are extremely strong and useful, but with the application of positional data in parallel to this, the sky is the limit! I strongly favor a combination of the two. Already now, the event-data are creating knowledge central to understanding the game at a different level than earlier (although it can be difficult to make this transparent to the coaches and scouts—a key issue). With positional data it will first of all be possible to use the event-data even better, especially in terms of evaluating the importance of the different events. The data will be instrumental in developing a basic structure for interpreting all other data, which again will make it easier to increase the transparency and understanding for all involved parties. For me this is one of the big potentials of positional data. In addition, a number of other types of analyses can be applied, but no more comments on this.

References

Biermann, C. (February 18, 2015). Moneyball im Niemandsland. *11 Freunde, 163.*
Biermann, C. (April 27, 2013). Der beste Profiwetter der Welt. *11 Freunde, 137.*
De Hoog, M. (March 24, 2015). How data, not people, call the shots in Denmark. *The Correspondent.* Retrieved from: https://thecorrespondent.com/2607/how-data-not-people-call-the-shots-in-denmark/230219386155-d2948861

7
WHERE ARE THEY RUNNING?

INTERVIEW WITH BAYERN MUNICH'S FITNESS GURU
DR. HOLGER BROICH

According to Lars Christensen, positional data offer almost unlimited opportunities especially in tactical terms. But application possibilities cannot only be limited to the field of match analysis. With an eye to practice, it becomes apparent that the application of data in the physical area is currently comparatively well established. In the subsequent chapters we will solely attend to the fascinating possibilities in the field of tactical analysis. However, before that we will see how performance diagnostics benefit from the new source of fitness data available today, especially if these are equipped with all kinds of additional sensor technology as in the case of wearable devices. Dr. Holger Broich, head of health and fitness of Bayern Munich, gives us a first insight.

Dr. Holger Broich is DFB-A-license coach and did his doctorate at the German Sport University Cologne about "Quantitative procedures for performance diagnostics in competitive football—empirical studies and evaluations of various performance-affecting parameters." From 2003 to 2014 he directed the sports scientific department of the Bayer 04 Leverkusen Fußball GmbH as a fitness coach and performance diagnostician (license department), and since 2014 he has directed the department of health and fitness of FC Bayern Munich (license department).

Dr. Broich, how can positional data help in the acquisition of physical performances?

I have used such data for many years, at the time at Bayer 04 Leverkusen and now at FC Bayern. The sum of all data is barely utilizable. For FC Bayern, we have undertaken a selection and aggregation about which I cannot give any information.

Various producers of wearable tracking devices provide data of other sensors next to the positional data such as heart rate measurements. How are these utilized in practice?

I use GPSports, almost in every training session along with real time measurements. In terms of data, the same holds true like I have just mentioned. There is simply no resilient offer of the companies or valid scientific insights about the integration.

Do the data nevertheless help in training control?

Of course, we collect all of these data for training control; otherwise they would not make sense. However, a recipe is not and will never be available. Rather expertise is sought here.

Can the measurements from training be transferred to competition anyways?

Competition and training must be seen as a unity, of course. As far as it is technically possible and physically or physiologically sensible, we use comparable data.

Are there already models currently available that make the players' load measurable and verifiable?

We use a self-developed model that also includes load markers.

The companies also promise to prevent injuries with suitable models and specific training control. How do you look upon the current development in this field?

An extremely important topic, which is discussed extensively as well in scientific literature and big studies, for example of the UEFA. But the state of facts is still not sufficient.

Making loads measurable

As seen in the interview, the keyword therefore is: load. How many kilometers a player ran (Carling, Bloomfield, Nelson, & Reilly, 2008), how many sprints s/he did, and what top speed s/he reached are useful data in sports coverage; for the professional players' medical staff it is, however, especially a matter of a purposeful load control of individual athletes and early warning systems in case of signs of fatigue.

This is for a good reason, since several injuries could be prevented if the players' exhaustion was better assessed. This was the key argument that finally moved the IFAB to permit wearable technology during official matches. In the end, these are solely designed for the players' benefit. The professionals' health is believed to be protected better with targeted load controls.

That is the rationale. What are lacking in practice though, are scientifically sound models, which can offer the suitable frame for a useful load control. Every player has highly individual physical preconditions and reacts extremely differently to physical activity at and above the threshold. Therefore there is and will be no panacea, as Broich also highlights. But how do, seen generally, indicators of fatigued players look like anyway? Which metrics provide information about how fast a player can be introduced to his routine comprising high loads after an injury? At this point in time, neither sports science nor sports medicine can give a satisfactory answer to this question (Drust, Atkinson, & Reilly, 2007; Carling, Bloomfield, Nelsen, & Reilly, 2008).

Therefore, the clubs are still mostly on their own. Nevertheless, they use the new methods concerning physical performance diagnostics, as the data source is just too valuable. Each team and every fitness staff has developed its own approach and, coupled with individual experience, they provide the current, optimal approach to efficient methods for controlling training and competitive loads.

However, none of the professional clubs wants to give insights into the exact procedures. In the end, they always hope also for a competitive advantage from the application of innovative analyses. The business is too big to expose potential progress in every area. Like Holger Broich, Lars Christensen would not reveal any details. And Ernst Tanner, too, did not want to give information on demand. This clearly shows how tightly drawn are the boundaries of helpfulness in modern football.

INTERVIEW WITH PROF. DR. LOCHMANN, SPORTS SCIENTIST, DOCTOR, AND UEFA A-LICENSE COACH

To what extent the great promises of running performances, heart rates, and acceleration metrics will come true in the end, remains to be seen. And even if science still cannot offer reliable models yet, it is still worthwhile to direct one's attention towards research. We spoke to Prof. Dr. Matthias Lochmann, who gives a scientific perspective on the topic in the interview.

Prof. Dr. Matthias Lochmann is a sports scientist, sports physician, and UEFA A-license coach. Since 2008, he has been working as professor at the Institute of Sport Science and Sport of the University of Erlangen-Nuremberg, and directs the working group of sports and exercise medicine there. He himself played football, among other clubs at SV Darmstadt 98. He acted as coach at the young talent training center of the 1. FSV Mainz 05 and at many other clubs. Matthias Lochmann was also involved in the development and implementation of the certification of German professional clubs' young talent training centers. In association with Fraunhofer-Gesellschaft, he worked on innovations in the field of data-driven competition and training control in real time. The possibilities and boundaries of competitive systems of periodization constitute a research focus for young athletes' development of performance and health.

Dear Prof. Dr. Lochmann, how are positional data used in medical and physical performance analysis?

Positional data can be used for the acquisition of the physical load from a performance physiological point of view. The individual strain of a football player is strictly delimited from this. It describes the individual reaction of the organism to the load and is depending on fitness level, age, recovery level and climate. Hence, similar load structures can have a different impact on one and the same person and especially between different persons. For the deduction of appropriate measures for training control and for the management of regeneration, an integral analysis of the load and the strain structure always has to follow. The isolated analysis of positional data inevitably leads to completely wrong conclusions.

Are there already data sources that suffice for day-to-day work?

A valid capture of the load and strain structure requires a reliable acquisition of positional data as well as a linked synchronous analysis of positional data and additional sensory data. This results from the aspect that for example the video-based analysis of positional data still has considerable deficiencies of reliability concerning temporal and spatial features. In GPS based methods, these deficiencies are even more distinct. By the addition of data from accelerometers, these deficiencies of reliability can be diminished. A radio location based local analysis of positional data corresponding to the state of the art can resolve the positional data with high temporal resolution, however, an error in the spatial resolution of plus or minus 5–10 cm remains here as well.

You have already addressed sensor technology, such as acceleration sensors incorporated in wearable tracking devices. Do these also help in the subsequent analysis, besides increasing the accuracy of the data?

The temporally synchronous measurement of the heart rate can provide valuable hints for the acquisition of the strain of the cardiovascular system.

If current reference data from performance physiological laboratory investigations are available, also assessments referring to the metabolic strain of the organism can be made.

Where are the difficulties here?

If practically relevant measures for the control of training and competition are supposed to follow from the recording and analysis of positional data, acceleration data and heart rate data, several aspects are required: first, the ability to capture valid, reliable and objective data and promptly—at best in real time—evaluate them. Furthermore, the capacity to run the data acquisition and assessment as gapless as possible in training and competition and also to make them available. And last but not least, the ability to ideally intermesh training, competition and regeneration management on the basis of the captured data.

Where has this concept been working most successfully to date in its implementation in practice?

In a methodically correct procedure, the load measurement is that area, which has been best manageable yet. An adequately applicable strain measurement turns out to be essentially more elaborate and more difficult. Deficiencies in the mentioned conditions pose the greatest obstacle for a sound, data-driven control of training, competition and regeneration even in numerous professional clubs worldwide.

A further problem is the lacking availability of appropriate, scientifically sound models, which could facilitate a data-driven control of training measures, preventive and rehabilitative measures in practice. As a result, it will at best be proceeded according to *best practice* even in 2017.

References

Carling, C., Bloomfield, J., Nelsen, L., & Reilly, T. (2008). The role of motion analysis in elite soccer: Contemporary performance measurement techniques and work rate data. *Sports Medicine, 38(10)*, 839–862.

Drust, B., Atkinson, G., & Reilly, T. (2007). Future perspectives in the evaluation of the physiological demands of soccer. *Sports Medicine, 37(9)*, 783–805.

8
FROM MEDIA TO STORYTELLING

Exercises at the touchscreen

"The ball is round and the match takes 90 minutes," is one of the best known quotes of Germany's record-holding national coach and icon Sepp Herberger. Down to the present day, nothing has changed in this principle of football, omitting added time and overtime for a moment. However, the media sequel, which the referee initiates with the final whistle, is new.

Therefore, today every match has a sequel—in television and at the news stands. Whoever wants to, can spend once again at least exactly as much time on the subsequent match analysis as on the live event before. Regarding television broadcasts, tactical contemplations during the half-time break and after the end of the game are meanwhile more compulsory than voluntary: whether Erik Meijer at the pay-TV channel Sky or Holger Stanislawski at ZDF, the demonstration of characteristic moves, formation faults, or pivotal moments at huge touchscreens has become common practice. With the match day analysis on Sport1, in fact, there has arisen over recent years a separate format for the tactical reprocessing of each Bundesliga match day.

Always in the line-up of the media third half: data. By no means is it only about the repetition of match events, but about new perspectives on the game. On the Internet, the opportunities for viewers are still more involved. Next to alternative camera perspectives, extensive information about the match is also available on the webpages of the broadcasting stations while the game is in progress. Furthermore, untold possibilities, for example the division's website www.bundesliga.de or the online portal of the sports news magazine *Kicker*, are available to explore interactively through the jungle of information.

This development has not come by chance but reflects an enormously increased demand from many football fans who are interested in more than just the goal scorers in the post-game reporting. By means of data-based facts, they are offered a completely new access to the background of the games and are provided with profound explanations for their tactical aspects. In addition, there is the optical component, as visually appealing charts can be created by positional data, raising sports coverage to a new level.

The heat map phenomenon

Taking a closer look though, the way in which data are dealt with seems still to be slightly clumsy here and there. Statistics on ball possession or pass completion rates, firmly established in the modern football commentator's vocabulary, are regularly used as a quality measures, even though they are evidentially no criterion for success. The higher a player's pass completion rate, the better, no question. But not always is the whole truth to be found in this metric. Among others, it ignores whether a player predominantly plays safe passes over short distances or whether s/he tries to expand the play with distinctly riskier passes.

Regarding ball possession rate, the same problem remains. This indicator gives a rough estimate of the dominance of each team, but rarely about their chances of winning. We will look into this more closely in subsequent chapters, but as Prof. Jürgen Perl's modelings show, only an extremely high percentage on the field in terms of ball possession increases the probability of a victory—figures below this magic 70 per cent threshold even display a tendency in the opposite direction.

Nevertheless, in sports coverage one can see again and again that, based on their ball possession rate, teams are labeled as "better" or "worse" or that defeats are called undeserved. Not only scientific findings are ignored in these cases, but also the employment of playing philosophies that deliberately relinquish excessive ball possession.

This disparity between illusion and reality can be seen best in the example of the classical heat map (Figure 8.1). For the data-affine football fan, it is an attractive eye catcher—however, it reveals very little about an individual player's behavior. One problem posed is the wide range of information that overlaps in the heat map depiction. The sum of all paths, irrespective of the context, creates a result that allows one at best to distinguish between, for instance, defensive and offensive midfield players.

Ultimately, you cannot really blame the broadcasting companies for this. Solving the problem of appropriate information visualization, which should ideally illustrate complex relations unambiguously, concisely, and vividly, is not easy, especially in the environment of an entertaining sportscast. Finally, the handling of match data is new ground for all parties involved and it would be wrong to fuel unrealistic expectations. It will take some time until the general understanding of progressive key performance indicators will grow and become established in the media landscape.

Yet, the fascination remains. Today, we may delight in additional statistical information and optical delicacies every week, no matter whether our favorite team is winning or not. Prospectively, further innovative and creative solutions will be developed and significantly influence the media experience of football.

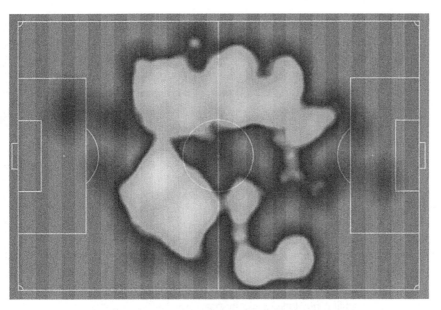

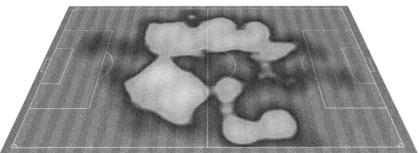

FIGURE 8.1A AND B Classic heat map

INTERVIEW WITH TIM BAGNER, CHYRONHEGO

Next to the broadcasting stations, diverse third-party suppliers are significantly involved in this development. One of these service providers is ChyronHego, specializing in media charts and a market leader in terms of acquiring positional data. Next to various European top divisions like the English Premier League, this Swedish-American company has also provided the Bundesliga with positional data since 2013. For this, Tim Bagner became Key Account Manager of ChyronHego GmbH (New York, Stockholm, and Cologne) in January 2013 and is responsible for match analysis and player scouting for the DFL—Deutsche Fußball Liga.

In this context, he provides the DFL with positional data. In June 2012 he started his position as UEFA Venue Operations & Broadcast Manager (and mentor) for the UEFA Champions League, UEFA Europa League, and European Qualification Games for the company UEFA Event S.A. in Nyon, Switzerland. Since May 2013 he has been both owner and managing director of the film and TV contract production GBS—German broadcast services, Germany. In the interview he gives a glimpse into the work behind the television cameras and collaboration with the Bundesliga.

Dear Mr. Bagner, data-driven match analysis enjoys more and more popularity on TV. As a media expert, how would you judge this development?

Media entrepreneurs such as Sky Germany, RTL, and the public channels are always looking for innovative products to increase the live experience for the audience and specially to make themselves stand out from non-linear competition. Sport as a live event with these high audience numbers offers the best profiling possibilities for the programs.

After the transition from HDTV to 4K, a groundbreaking development for camera systems is currently not in sight. Innovations in the media sector, especially in live reporting, will rather concentrate on the area of match analysis. The use of data in the media for match analysis will successively increase in the following years.

How would you explain this hype?

On the one hand, this is because the recording systems for live data are becoming more elaborate, more precise, and faster. On the other hand, positional data are fed with more scouting information, so that the possibility of a substantial analysis during live broadcasting—may it be during the game, during commercials, during halftime or after the game—increases.

What possibilities can be offered to broadcsasters by the current flood of data?

Thanks to the rapid development of graphical processor performances extensive and expensive applications can be calculated quicker and be presented to the audience or user in a diverse and prompt manner. Either as live element in a show, for example virtual animation as 1st or 2nd replay with changes of perspective, or as 2nd screen applications with virtual reality options for the spectator on the couch. Live positional data without latency but with high quality and validity will play a decisive role for all applications and animations in the future.

Are there any other fields of application apart from graphical processing?

Next to the virtual application of match scenes, live positional data will also deliver important information on more precise and qualitative match scene analyses. In the future, every result of a match analysis will be supported by "hard data facts." The data underpin the analysis and with the help of data key situations will automatically be recognized—keyword pattern recognition.

As market leader, ChyronHego works globally in terms of player tracking and has served the 1st and 2nd Bundesliga since 2013. Which prerequisites must a data collector have nowadays to equip a European top league?

The distribution of recording rights depends on many factors. The clubs come first with their need to receive reliable data of high quality during the game, so they can make ad hoc decisions such as replacement due to condition limits, injury prevention or change of tactics and so on.

In the post analyses, the data should be ready as soon as possible, to use these for visual applications. What counts here is delivering 100 per cent valid positional data for players and the ball in no time. But the sole collection of positional data does not suffice nowadays to supply complete leagues.

What else is important?

There are many startups, which can and want to refine the data in many ways. But a minimum of qualitative evaluations is expected by all clubs, especially as financially weak clubs cannot run own positional data evaluations. Furthermore, refinancing models strongly depend on data depth, not only from data quality. That's why all data providers are required to run additional refinements, to increase data utility. Positional data deliver a lot more information that running distances and speed.

In Germany, all teams in the 1st and 2nd Bundesliga have complete access to these data and can thus use the data of opposing teams for their analyses. Can this situation be compared to other European leagues?

Currently, every league is pursuing another concept. At the beginning, there is the question of who receives which data and who owns the data. In some leagues, such as the ones in England, the league association EPL assigns the data collector, similar to the situation in Germany. However, only the two teams of the respective game receive the data. In other leagues, all clubs have access to the data of every league fixture. The data owner decides which data can be processed in which way. The live data quality also varies with the respective league concept and the selected data collector.

How is that?

Of course, the available budget also decides on the data quality and depth of data processing. There are two-dimensional systems not recording the ball and there are three-dimensional systems recording ball data and furthermore information such as net playing time, ball possession, pass behavior, ball control behavior during the live process. Additionally, seasonal data banks are handled differently. Some leagues work without databanks and leave this to third-party suppliers.

Television channels often afford tracking systems to offer their spectators more content for selected matches and to work with live data. In the Netherlands, there is the channel Fox for example that is working with live positional data to both generate common statistics from the data and especially to create virtual realities. Even in Japan the league's tracking partner is a media business, for whom providing the clubs with data comes second.

So, central data collection is currently only a phenomenon in the big leagues?

In many average and small leagues the respective clubs assign their data collector, contracts across leagues are only made within the big leagues.

Is there any explanation for this?

In the different leagues, the refinancing possibilities are very different from one another. But there is the clear trend that more and more average and small leagues also go for larger league decisions. The Belgian and Dutch leagues have now decided to introduce a tracking system across the league. This is due to the progressing professionalization of the leagues and further to the economic potential of the data. Statistics can be used in all forms of media and the data trade is easy and scalable.

The latest technical developments have focused mainly on a method of reliably tracking the ball. How important is ball tracking?

Ball tracking is becoming increasingly important to provide profound tactical analyses in real time next to the performance data. Ball speed and ball distances within the team ball possession sequences are an extremely important parameter for example to clearly show pass security, pass rates and playing efficiency. With the development towards 4K Tracking the ball can be recorded even more accurately. However, the ball position often still needs to be calculated, as the ball can be covered by the players.

It is not always possible to deduce the ball position from the image analysis of the camera signals at hand. The necessary calculation—where was the ball in the last frame, in which radius could the ball be in the current frame, where can the ball impossibly be?—Already takes place during the determination of the ball position. At a frame rate of 25, the ball additionally needs speed filters, to present valid speed values for every single frame. This leads to a latency, which makes it useful only for a few live systems.

Which systems nevertheless work for ball position?

For example, ball positions deliver nowadays the trigger signal for audio mixing consoles in broadcasting vehicles. With an increasing number of microphones, currently the minimal standard for football broadcasting is twelve microphones at the pitch, an audio engineer cannot offer a reasonable audio mix containing every ball contact anymore. Live ball data helps to control audio fader completely automatically.

In the future, automatic pan-tilt head cameras will be directed by positional data of the ball. The pan-scan technology uses high-resolving static camera images, 4K or 8K, but only small sections based on positional data are generated. This becomes necessary for fully automated television productions of sport events.

9

KEY PROPERTIES OF LONG-TERM SUCCESS IN FOOTBALL

Introduction

In modern football, underdog success stories are no rarity. Take for example Borussia Mönchengladbach's qualification for the UEFA Champions League in 2015, around four years after the club just avoided relegation. Or, during the same season, how FC Augsburg sensationally qualified for the Europa League as well.

FIGURE 9.1 Borussia Mönchengladbach's players celebrate with their fans after an important victory over VfL Wolfsburg on their way to securing a spot in the UEFA Champions League (2015)

Source: Patrik Stollarz/AFP/Getty Images

One year before that, it was 1. FSV Mainz 05 that unexpectedly made it into European football, and in the season before, both Eintracht Frankfurt and SC Freiburg. Repeatedly, alleged underdogs manage to stun experts with their achievements and excite their fans, even over a longer period of time. As did Leicester City, winning the English Premier League in 2016.

On a slightly more general note, which team finishes where at the end of a season in terms of table position is closely linked to the question of how such over-performances can be explained. To this end, the comparison to circumstances like the financial standing of a club has already been drawn more frequently and a correlation can't be denied (Frick, 2005; Heuer, 2012). But is it also possible to explain the team's differences in performance on a tactical level?

From Gladbach's point of view, the path from close-to-relegation to becoming an international contestant was a development over several years, closely linked to the workings of the then head coach Favre. Under his charge, the team tried repeatedly to enter the opposing penalty box by attacking down the flanks with very offensive wingbacks, but also managed to effectively pass through the center with the help of strong strikers, Raffael and Kruse. In the 2014–2015 season, besides Gladbach, FC Bayern Munich, VfL Wolfsburg, and Bayer 04 Leverkusen also secured places in the Champions League. Looking at the teams' different playing philosophies, it is easy to recognize that quite diverse styles helped those teams to the top of the table.

Alongside Gladbach, VfL Wolfsburg also played a game characterized by pressing in midfield while relying on quick counterattacks. Leverkusen, in contrast, became well known for their extremely aggressive offensive pressing. On the other side of the spectrum, FC Bayern effectively constricted the opponents to their own penalty box by their dominant, ball-oriented play and patiently waited for gaps to open up. Four teams, four philosophies—and all of them reached the top in the end. Although the search for an explanation for this diversity of success strategies implied especially subjectively conducted debates to date, novel techniques and methods of automated game analysis nowadays also provide objective insights on the basis of positional data (for an overview see Memmert, Lemmink, & Sampaio, 2017).

Large-scale analysis of the fundamental question

For a well-founded scientific analysis, it needs to be considered that a lot can happen in 90 minutes of a single match and that the final score does not always accurately reflect the relative strength of the two teams on the pitch. Yet, after completing all 34 matches in the season, the 18 teams of the Bundesliga usually find themselves at a position in the table that correctly mirrors their playing ability during the season—compared to their competitors.

Focusing exclusively on the team's tactical performance, as mentioned at the start of the chapter, it is possible to analyze how successful teams are characterized by their playing performance, and which similarities they show despite different playing styles. In a recent study, researchers devoted themselves to exactly this question (Memmert et al., 2016a, 2016b). The performance data of teams in the upper and lower thirds of the table in the Bundesliga were compared according to the final table of season 2014–2015. The Big-Data field study, to which the results in the following chapters mainly refer, included a total of 50 games comprising of over 310,000,000 data points from over 4,200 minutes of football played in the German top flight.

The aforementioned match analysis tool SOCCER (© Perl, 2011) was employed and eventually 11,160 computed performance indicators were evaluated, complemented by traditional, manually created match analyses.

Comparing the performances of both groups regarding progressed KPIs by different statistical tests, the results show a markedly greater dominance of teams with more playing ability. In the evaluation, an especially distinct superiority in measurements concerning one of the newly designed KPIs comes to the fore: control of spaces. As we will see, this value is distinctly in favor of the top teams.

A geometric approach to the concept of spatial control

Before we take a closer look at the results, first it should be noted how a performance indicator of spatial control can be defined. In a first intuitive description, each player would be assigned exactly that space on the field that he can reach before any other players due to their current position. Nevertheless, players differ regarding their individual physical conditions, as for example in acceleration or agility. Situational factors such as the current running direction can additionally play a role.

These personal factors are hard to determine even though scientists have been doing research on suitable motion models. Yet, experience shows that, on the one hand, potential inequalities balance each other out by the interaction of the players in a team and, on the other hand, over the course of 90 minutes. Therefore, it is simply assumed that each player controls those parts of the field to which he is closest. Statistically speaking this simplification does not have to be a disadvantage. If a general model detects underlying effects, it provides a valuable basis for refinements.

The basis for the technical realization of this idea is provided by the Ukrainian mathematician Georgi Feodosjewitsch Voronoi, who published his thoughts more than 100 years ago (Voronoi, 1907). His approach allows for the geometrical partitioning of the field in 22 areas, the so-called Voronoi diagram. This partitioning regards every player as the center of a cell that exactly covers the surface of the playing field containing the points that are closest to him. The border of two adjacent cells is therefore drawn at the point that both players can reach at the same time. In the easiest and most basic case there are just two players controlling two different spaces depending on their positions on the field. However, it already becomes more complicated with five players (Figure 9.2).

By using Voronoi cells, which formally refer to a theoretical concept for identifying spheres of influence, it is determined which area on the field is controlled by every player during a certain period of time (e.g., first or second half). More

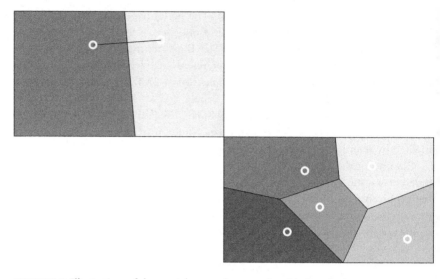

FIGURE 9.2 Illustration of the spatial control approach with 2 or 5 players.

practically it results in a percentage value, determined by the sum of the points that some players reach faster than others. In order to analyze the offensive play of a team, it is of particular interest how much control they create and manage in the critical zones in the offense (Perl & Memmert, 2017).

Therefore, the main focus in the study is on the offense zone and the penalty areas rather observing the whole pitch. Furthermore, primarily passes were considered. That way it was possible to examine how spatial control values shift when one team is in possession of the ball: How do they manage to take over and retain the critical areas of the field during their own passing game?

The following situation is supposed to clarify the concept of spatial control on the pitch. The Figure 9.3 presents a situation from the match Werder Bremen vs. 1. FC Köln, from the ninth match day of the above-mentioned season. In Figure 9.4, a two-dimensional representation of the same situation is demonstrated, on which the calculated Voronoi diagram is additionally interpolated. The image shows Bremen (yellow) in possession, with Makiadi passing the ball to Bartels. At this point Werder are controlling 31.5 per cent of their attacking zone and 1.6 per cent of the opposing penalty area. In addition, they are able to gain 6 and 11 percentage points in the attacking zone and penalty area, respectively.

Top-rated teams dominate in terms of spatial control

In order to investigate the differences between higher and lower placed teams, all played passes of both groups were compared to each other. It became apparent that the top teams achieved markedly greater spatial gains, especially with the passing game in the attacking zone. Especially if the ball was played within the

In a recent research project (Rein et al., 2017; Memmert & Rein, 2018, in press) vertical passes to the offense in an attempt to create spatial control were analyzed. Passing behavior is a key property of successful performance in team sport games. However, previous approaches have mainly focused on total passing frequency in relation to game outcomes. which provides little information about what actually constitutes successful passing behavior. This affects the application of these findings by practitioners. In that study, two novel approaches to are presented in assessing passing effectiveness in elite football, by evaluating changes in majority situations in front of the goal and changes in space dominance due to passing behavior. Majority situations were evaluated by calculating the number of opposing players between the ball carrier and the goal, whereas space dominance was assessed using Voronoi cells. The application of both methods to exemplary positional data from twelve German 1st Bundesliga matches demonstrates that they capture different features of passing behavior. The results further show that on average, passes made from the midfield into the attacking area are more effective than passes within the attacking area. The present approaches provide interesting new avenues for future applications in more depth, with immediate value for practitioners, for example, with respect to tactical training regimes or when following up performance, as the routines allow rapid identification of individual passes. The routines are also applicable to other sport disciplines.

FIGURE 9.3 Situation in the game between Werder Bremen and 1. FC Köln

Source: © DFL—Deutsche Fußball Liga GmbH

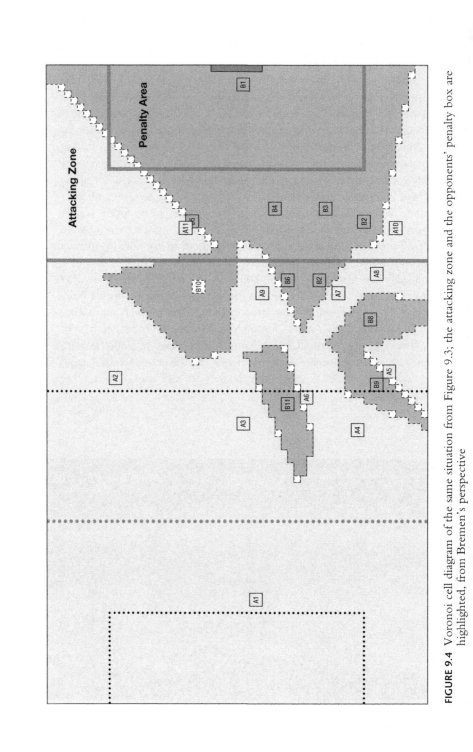

FIGURE 9.4 Voronoi cell diagram of the same situation from Figure 9.3; the attacking zone and the opponents' penalty box are highlighted, from Bremen's perspective

defense or the midfield or was passed forward from the defense to the midfield and from the midfield to the offense, the difference between the top and bottom teams was clearly demonstrated.

However, that does not imply that teams dominate more than half of the attacking zone with their passing game. Rather, with a pass from the midfield to the attacking zone, for example, they can generally control wider areas than the relegation candidates in regard to comparable passes.

This tendency is also apparent in the opposing penalty box. Here, the teams that are at the top of the table on average control more space when passing in midfield and with passes back from the attacking to midfield zone. Moreover, by using various combinations in midfield, these teams are able to win space in the offensive area more efficiently—which are generally larger compared to the passes of the lesser teams.

Generally, it will be noted that top teams manage to gain and keep space in critical areas of the pitch more successfully. As noted, the way to the top can take different directions, indeed. However, apparently all of these directions are shaped strongly by characteristic tactical achievements, namely an efficient use of space.

A frequent key topic in the discussion of the most effective way of playing football is the question concerning ball possession. On a tactical level, such insights can add a new dimension to this question. They clearly show that next to the ball possession, it is equally important how a team understands to handle space when attacking—at least in order to perform successfully in the longer term.

References

Frick, B. (2005). '. . . Und Geld schießt eben doch Tore: Die Voraussetzungen sportlichen und wirtschaftlichen Erfolges in der Fußball-Bundesliga.' *Sportwissenschaft*, *35*, 250–270.

Heuer, A. (2012). *Der perfekte Tipp*. Weinheim: Wiley.

Memmert, D., Lemmink, K. A. P. M., & Sampaio, J. (2017). Current Approaches to Tactical Performance Analyses in Soccer using Position Data. *Sports Medicine*, *47*(1), 1–10. doi:10.1007/s40279-016-0562-5

Memmert, D., Raabe, D., Knyazev, A., Franzen, A., Zekas, L., Rein, R., . . . Weber, H. (2016a). Innovative Leistungsindikatoren im Profifußball auf Basis von Positionsdaten. *Impulse*, *2*, 14–21.

Memmert, D., Raabe, D., Knyazev, A., Franzen, A., Zekas, L., Rein, R., . . . Weber, H. (2016b). Big Data im Profi-Fußball. Analyse von Positionsdaten der Fußball-Bundesliga mit neuen innovativen Key Performance Indikatoren. *Leistungssport*, *46*(5), 21–26.

Memmert, D. & Rein, R. (2018, in press). Match analysis, Big Data and tactics: current trends in elite soccer. *German Journal of Sport Medicine*, *69*(3), 65–72.

Perl, J. & Memmert, D. (2017). A pilot study on offensive success in soccer based on space and ball control—key performance indicators and key to understand game dynamics. *International Journal of Computer Science in Sport*, *16*(1), 65–75. doi: 10.1515/ijcss-2017-0005.

Rein, R., Raabe, D., & Memmert, D. (2017). "Which pass is better?" Novel approaches to assess passing effectiveness in elite soccer. *Human movement science*, *55*, 172–181.

Voronoi, G. (1907). Nouvelles applications des parametres continus a la theorie des formes quadratiques. *Journal für Reine und Angewandte Mathematik*, *133*, 97–178.

10
THE KEY TO SUCCESS

New insights into the oldest of all questions

It is one of the simplest and oldest questions in football and the most difficult to answer at the same time: Which team hops into the shower as winner after 90 minutes? Or, simply, who wins? According to Gary Lineker, the Germans. According to sports science, the answer is not that easy, because the simplicity of the question makes an answer that difficult. The game by itself is broken down into its parts more and more successfully, and tactical aspects are determined and modeled increasingly precisely. As soon as all parts of this puzzle are pieced together, however, a broad picture shows up that is hard to make sense of.

As is generally known, chance also plays a role in the outcome of a match and furthermore severe mistakes by individual players undermine the most exact analyses. Thus, every now and then the underdog on paper emerges as the winner and the team that was superior, from an analytic perspective, leaves the pitch as the loser.

There are plenty of examples of this phenomenon, but maybe the most memorable in recent history occurred in Glasgow on November 7, 2012. The superior FC Barcelona were the away team at Celtic Park during the Champions League group stage, and were expected to dominate the home team theoretically. The Catalans claimed 25 shots to Celtic's 5, and held 84 per cent ball possession. In the end they were just 45 passes short of 1,000, coupled with a passing rate of 91 per cent—an outstanding statistic. For comparison, Celtic managed to execute no more than 166 successful passes, 38 per cent of all attempts missing the target. In the end, a safe 3–0 for Barcelona? Not this time!

Celtic beat the supposedly outstanding opponent 2–1, with Barcelona scoring their only goal courtesy of Lionel Messi in time added on (90+1 minutes). The surprise was perfect—David had brought the vastly superior Goliath to his knees.

FIGURE 10.1 Goalkeeper Yann Sommer watches as Leon Goretzka's deflected shot finds the net during Gladbach's away match at Schalke (2016)

Source: Dean Mouhtaropoulos/Bongarts/Getty Images

FIGURE 10.2 Marc Batra of Barcelona and Celtic's Captain, Georgios Samaras, fight for the ball during a UEFA Champions League group match at Celtic Park (2012)

Source: Jeff J Mitchell/Getty Images Sport/Getty Images

While this extreme example clearly does not tell the whole story of the wide-ranging match statistics such as pass completion rate, ball possession, or tackles won, the question remains: Which performance indicators eventually reflect the outcome of a game? For quite some time, scientists have been looking for typical characteristics of successful teams' style of play. However, as is well known, only a few goals are usually scored in football especially when compared to other sports. At worst, a single goal will decide the outcome.

In practice, this constitutes a major hurdle if attempting to connect the playing performance with the result. A solution to the problem is the use of very large samples, as in the case in the study discussed (Memmert et al., 2016; Memmert & Rein, 2018). When comparing data on winners and losers in a sufficiently large sample, distortions of individual matches increasingly fade into the background and the actual differences will come to light.

Yet, in practice, only a few features become apparent in games where weaker teams are inferior to their opponents. An analysis of several World Cups concluded that the number of shots on target alone could reliably differentiate between winning and losing teams (Castellano et al., 2012). Analyses from the Spanish League by Lago-Penas et al. (2010) also came to a similar conclusion. An initial indication, but not very revealing. It also appears that there is no direct connection between tackles won, distance covered, the number of corner kicks, and the final score.

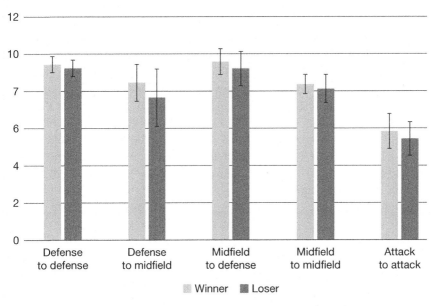

FIGURE 10.3 The winning team clearly has more spatial control in the opposition's 30 meter zone and penalty box than the inferior team, no matter whether the ball is played from defense, midfield, or attack

Passing like Özil

However, it is unknown whether teams differ from one another regarding advanced key performance indicators. Therefore, the performance data of winners and losers was compared in the present study in terms of newly designed KPIs. It turned out that there were marked differences, especially in regard to one performance indicator. Apart from elaborate calculations such as the examination of player movements, it is also simple to calculate, with the help of positional data, the number of players that are able to defend against the attacking team at a certain point in time.

Thus, it is possible to compute both the mean number of defending players and the number of outplayed opponents when teams play their passes. These indicators are strongly supported by exercise science, where passes that outplay many defense players are assigned high importance. Many coaches currently see long, vertical passes as the optimal solution to moving the ball rapidly into dangerous areas in front of the goal. Players such as Mesut Özil and their pinpoint passes are therefore more sought after than ever.

Positional data are in practice the ideal starting point to analyze long, vertical passes. In the blink of an eye, calculated information on outplayed opponents and remaining defenders is available. Especially the former is generally recognized as a quality criterion and serves as the basis for refined calculation, as for example *pressure efficiency*. But also, the contextual information is interesting: How many defensive players does a team still have behind the ball when the opposition plays a through ball?

Alongside fully automated answers to this question, positional data have yet another major advantage: objectivity. Imagine that Jérôme Boateng or Mats Hummels bend one of their famous long balls behind the opposition defensive line. They frequently outplay numerous opponents with their devastating use of the long through ball straight out of defense. Yet how do you judge the wing player on the far side of the field, for example? Obviously, he was still positioned between the central defender and pass receiver during the pass. But would he have been able to intervene even if the team had combined passes through the center? Should he be counted as being outplayed or does he only rate as extra in the current situation? Focusing on defenders would be the get-out-of-jail from this situation, but here also difficulties arise. How would you treat defensive midfield players in a team that is not positioned high up the pitch? Who counts as a defending player if individual players have situationally switched their role?

Again, it is geometry that provides the solution here, because in an automated calculation it is necessary to formally define which opponent can still defend in any given situation. Two different definitions were tested in the present study. First, an imaginary line parallel to the goal line separated the player who was playing the pass and the opponent's goal—which is the simplest variant. Everything between these lines belongs to the group of players who can still defend. Second, a circle was chosen instead of a line to exclude players at the periphery of the field.

Many other possibilities are also conceivable and the ideal formulation of this rule will emerge over time. However, it is obviously never going to cover all differing expert opinions in all situations. Yet, it is always going to be decided in the same way. Any inaccuracies caused by subjective assessments are then a thing of the past.

The game opener as the game changer

Let us return to the initial question. It has been found that in the above model of outplayed opposition, significant differences between the first and second winner at half-time can be seen in statistical procedures. By focusing on the opposition players that can still defend during a pass, the winning teams are on average confronted with fewer opposition players during all passes between and within their defense and their midfield.

On average, winning teams face fewer opposition players at the moment a pass is executed into the attacking zone, which constitutes an elementary field advantage. There are two additional differences: On the one hand, weaker teams outplay significantly fewer opponents when passing from defense to midfield. On the other hand, they face a greater number of defenders when playing into the attacking zone. Winning teams can therefore not only get more players behind the ball in when the opposition is on the attack, but also manage to outplay more opposition players during the initial part of the game.

Interestingly, this is a comparatively simple calculation that could throw light on the crucial question of triumph or defeat. It also confirms expert opinion regarding the importance of an efficient vertical game. The importance of passes into spaces is further underlined by the results from the information box in

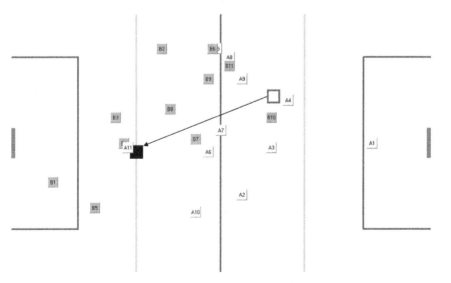

FIGURE 10.4 Diagram of a pass that outplays 6 opposition players at a stroke

Chapter 9, according to which through passes result in most gained space. Was Celtic's Fraser Forster aware of this when, in the 83rd minute, he played the ball past all 10 field players of FC Barcelona with a punt, and Tony Wade scored an easy second (and winning) goal? Most likely not. And for sure this did not interest the fans of Celtic on this memorable evening in November.

In the future, we will be able to determine exactly how well a team is able to neutralize the opposition's defensive lines or opens important spaces in forward movements. With scientifically validated key performance indicators, it will be possible to quantify, compare, and reevaluate the longstanding expertise of coaches. In terms of match analysis, an unknown level of depth can be achieved. Let us go a step further and deepen our investigation.

References

Castellano, J., Casamichana, D., & Lago, C. (2012). The use of match statistics that discriminate between successful and unsuccessful soccer teams. *Journal of Human Kinetics*, *31*, 139–147.

Lago-Penas, C., Lago-Ballesteros, J., Dellal, A., & Gomez, M. (2010). Game-related statistics that discriminated winning, drawing and losing teams from the Spanish soccer league. *Journal of Sports Science and Medicine*, *9*, 288–293.

Memmert, D., Raabe, D., Knyazev, A., Franzen, A., Zekas, L., Rein, R., . . . Weber, H. (2016). Innovative Leistungsindikatoren im Profifußball auf Basis von Positionsdaten. *Impulse*, *2*, 14–21.

Memmert, D. & Rein, R. (2018). Match analysis, Big Data and tactics: current trends in elite soccer. *German Journal of Sport Medicine*, *69*(3), 65–72.

11
REASONS FOR DOMINANCE

Giants' summit at Wembley

Only one day before Celtic's sensational victory against Barcelona, 1,700 km further south: In the Estadio Santiago Bernabéu, Barca's (FC Barcelona's) eternal rival Real Madrid encounters Borussia Dortmund, the then German champions (the "Black-Yellows") who are leading 2–1 in the final minute, when a certain Mesut Özil (Real) proved that, besides deadly passes, well-executed direct free kicks are also part of his repertoire. With the equalizer, he saved José Mourinho's team a point. But even with defeat, the disgrace would have been considerably less compared to what happened 24 hours later in Glasgow. After all, Borussia Dortmund had long ago become a team of international top-class players. The team coach Jürgen Klopp played thrilling football, which also had to be experienced again by Real Madrid when facing Dortmund later that season in the semi-final.

The story of Dortmund's success already began two years before, in the 2010–2011 season. Only six years after almost going bankrupt, they topped the Bundesliga with a young and promising team. In the following season, Borussia Dortmund dominated the league and won the first league/cup double in the club's history. In the following years, the fight for the championship in the Bundesliga developed mainly into a duel between BVB and FC Bayern Munich. As a side issue, a rivalry between both teams emerged, which reached its temporary summit at Wembley in 2013. Bayern had conquered Barcelona in the semi-final, and after Dortmund's triumph over Madrid it came to a well-matched final. Never had two German teams faced each other in a UEFA Champions League final.

Regarding the Bundesliga, both spectators and officials complained about the marked one-sidedness in the championship, comparing this to the situation in Spain where for several years usually either Real Madrid or Barcelona won the league. However, by winning the triple under Jupp Heynckes and the subsequent successes of Bayern under Pep Guardiola, tension at the top of the table in Germany decreased even more. Before long, Dortmund were no longer able to challenge Bayern seriously.

Not only in Germany or Spain do we find teams that dominate the league almost at will. In France's Ligue 1 there is Paris Saint-Germain and in Italy, Juventus have monopolized the title in recent years. For the fans, these series of triumphs may seem boring in the long run but it is worth looking at this more closely, because behind the seemingly effortless victories often lies a very strong tactical performance.

To find the reasons for this, it is worth continuing the comparison from the preceding chapter. This is possible due to analysis of those games in which one of the teams left the pitch as a clear winner. Thus, undeserved and lucky wins can, on the one hand, be largely ignored and the remaining games can, on the other hand, provide an even better basis for investigating the differences between winning and losing teams. The terms "clear" or "safe" are, however, very subjective and must be defined in a certain way. For this reason, the following analyses considered all halves that ended with a lead of two or more goals as a clear victory.

FIGURE 11.1 Franck Ribéry (Bayern Munich) and Marco Reus (Borussia Dortmund) during the 2013 UEFA Champions League final at Wembley (2013)

Source: Christian Liewig—Corbis/Corbis Sport/Getty Images

Whoever wins well does a lot of things right

Now, in contrast to the previous chapter, the number of outplayed opponents no longer turns out to be the main difference between the two groups. Here it is a mix of different factors that favor the winning team. They have key advantages, especially when passing from the defense to the midfield, in other words during the early part of the game: Not only are more opposition players outplayed by the winning team with these passes, but the winners also dominate greater areas in the attacking zone. With passes into this area, more space can be acquired as well. In addition, the superiority of passes in the attacking zone becomes noticeable. Superior teams manage to dominate greater space in both the attacking zone and the opposition's penalty box with their passes (Figure 11.3).

In addition, winning teams show faster organization after losing the ball. This phenomenon can be attributed to another key performance indicator, the so-called pressing index. With this calculation the defensive switchovers of a team are recorded: How quickly do the players manage to fill the space around the opponent who controls the ball?

The mean velocity of all players located close to the ball is decisive when calculating this indicator. Measurements are taken at two different points in time: three seconds after loss of possession (t1) and after the ball has travelled a specific distance (t2) (Figure 11.2). By this, both the spatial and temporal aspects of turnover are considered. According to this analysis, winning teams are especially dominant regarding point t1. More precisely, they regroup distinctly more rapidly after losing the ball compared to inferior teams.

In summary, it can be stated that teams which win by a two-goal margin are characterized in particular by their effective passing to the midfield, good spatial gains regarding passes to the offense, and a better changeover performance in defense. Particularly in respect of outplayed opposition players, a clear pattern can be realized compared with the findings from the previous chapters: The obvious prevalence of winning teams in positional play ranges over all passes, irrespective of their origin and destination. The key performance indicators, based on the outplayed and yet to be outplayed opposition players, can be key important factors regarding victory or defeat.

Therefore, a lot of things need to happen for an empathic victory. Good turnover behavior in the defense, effective vertical play in the build-up game, and space-opening passes in the offense. What sounds like a brilliant tactical achievement is all the more difficult to implement on the pitch. Nevertheless, teams like Bayern and Dortmund manage to meet these challenges almost in every game—an enormously impressive performance, even if many matches appear to the spectators to be more like a test match.

As we have seen, positional data present new opportunities to describe these performances objectively. They help us find answers to the most basic questions in the game and sharpen our comprehension of tactical performance. But how do these new methods perform in a more limited context? Can they be advantageous to us in individual fixtures? Let's find out!

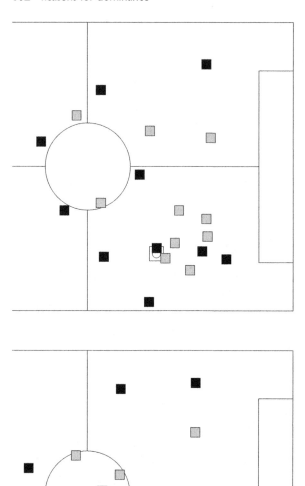

FIGURE 11.2A, B, C AND D A dynamic process analysis with a precise time selection as a measure of pressing speed in football (from left to right). The ball (circle in a square) and its trajectory are shown. Team A (black squares) lose the ball and all players from that team try to get it back from Team B (gray squares) as fast as they can. The process speed is calculated (in m/s) to show how fast each player is moving towards the ball. For the variable "pressing speed," the process speed average—in terms of a team effort—can be checked.

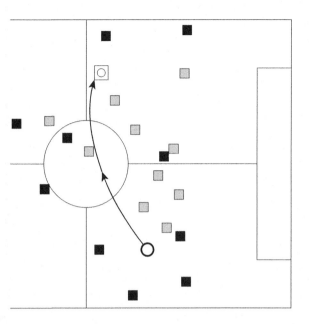

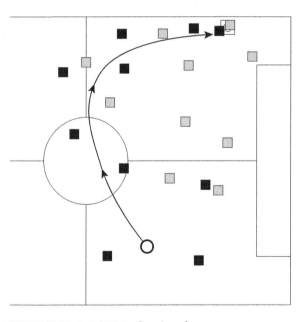

FIGURE 11.2A, B, C AND D Continued

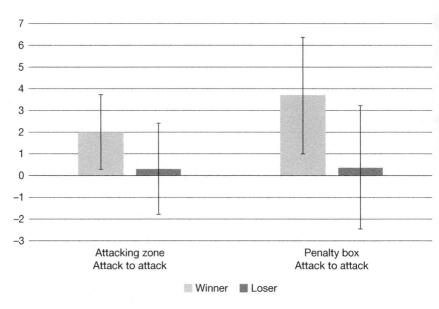

FIGURE 11.3 The team that won by two goals clearly had more spatial control in the opposition's 30 meter zone and penalty box than the losing team, no matter whether the ball is played from defense, midfield, or attack. Better pressing can be observed as well.

12

FCB VERSUS FCB

Duel in the Champions League

In its treble-winning season 2012–2013, FC Bayern Munich beat FC Barcelona 7–0 on aggregate in the semi-final of the Champions League. But not in all encounters with the Catalans has the momentum been so obviously with the Germans. Many of the duels between FCB and FCB were considerably more balanced, with Barca dominating in some.

One of these occasions was in 2009, when these football heavyweights faced each other in the Champions League quarter-final. After a 4–0 defeat in the first leg, Bayern coach Jürgen Klinsmann's team already had their backs to the wall. Especially in the first half, the German champions' restructured defense had major problems with the trio of Thierry Henry, Samuel Eto'o, and Lionel Messi in attack. Indeed, they had to accept defeat in the first leg and were in no great position for the second one. The chances of winning on aggregate had shrunk dramatically.

Yet Pep Guardiola, coach of the Catalans at that time, warned against this allegedly comfortable situation: "We have one foot in the semi-final, but we take Bayern very seriously. We have no right to think that we are already out of danger just because we won the first leg. We have a comfortable advantage, but anything can happen in sport." In the meantime, coach Klinsmann tried to mobilize his forces: "It would be unrealistic to claim that we will make it, but we will try everything to win the return game. We showed too much respect in Barcelona; some of my players seemed to be plainly overwhelmed."

The comeback of both the sadly missed Lúcio and Philipp Lahm was a silver lining for Munich, hoping to regain stability in defense. However, neither Miroslav Klose nor Bastian Schweinsteiger could help their team in this upcoming mammoth task as both were injured. Nevertheless, Klinsmann talked a combative game: "All of us are now more stable and more self-confident. We want to show breathtaking football and to bow out of the Champions League with dignity."

FIGURE 12.1 Champions League, 2008–2009 quarter-final, FC Bayern Munich versus FC Barcelona (1–1)

Source: John Macdougall/AFP/Getty Images

In the end, FC Bayern only managed a 1–1 draw against the eventual winner of the competition. This Champions League match of the titans will serve as our basis in presenting a positional data-based post-match analysis that could be expected in the future. Even today, it would be possible to implement this analysis online during the match.nowadays, technological requirements are replacing subjective assessment for a range of tactical performance indicators by computer-based, scientific analysis methods, or at least are complementing them. Through the use of of positional data, analyses can be conducted in just a few seconds, ideally in real time.

How would such a scenario appear? The basic idea is that neuronal networks, as developed by Jürgen Perl's and Daniel Memmert's research group (Memmert & Perl, 2006, 2009a, 2009b; Grunz, et al., 2009, 2012; Memmert et al., 2011; Perl & Memmert, 2011, 2012; Perl et al., 2013), allow comparison of situations from single or multiple matches. From this, it can be deduced which formations the players typically adopted on the pitch and which effects resulted from their positioning in each case. For example, all permutations of a short game opening are to be recognized by the neuron-cluster "short game opening."

The advantage over previous methods is that the identification of playing sequences from football matches does no longer has to be accomplished manually (conventional analysis), but can be done by neuronal networks automatically and almost in real time. This allows for classification of enormous amounts of data within a few minutes according to differences and similarities (Figure 12.2).

An essential aspect of the assessment of teams' tactical behavior is the interaction between specific tactical groups, like offense and defense, for example. Yet, it is problematic that despite the availability of positional data, the analysis—for instance of tactical movements of player formations—is hardly realizable with conventional methods, simply because of the previously mentioned immense data volumes. Here, the abilities of neuronal networks to recognize patterns offer essential new opportunities as indicated in Figure 12.2. Formations can be separated from their position on the field and can be identified by the system as characteristic formations. This makes it possible to determine frequency distributions of typical formations and to recognize temporal courses of tactical team interactions.

For validation of the trained neuronal networks, the results from traditional match analysis ("gold standard") on the one hand and from the net-based match analysis based on positional data on the other hand, were compared. In initial studies, it became apparent (Grunz et al., 2012) that almost 90 per cent of the match events recognized by traditional match analysis were detected by neuronal networks regarding various group tactics like game opening, set-play (more differentiated for throw-ins, free kicks, and corners) and goals.

Down to the present day, further optimizing steps have taken place, at which congruency rates of over 95 per cent were achieved. Considering that experts on average show a congruity of 80 per cent regarding tactics that are difficult to define, such as the game opening, the importance of computer-based analysis methods becomes clear.

Let's return to the above-mentioned match between FC Bayern Munich and FC Barcelona. Based on preprocessed positional data, a match protocol can be created automatically listing player–ball interactions to the exact second: ball contacts, receipts, passes, possession wins, possession, and possession losses. The protocol entries can now be used for various analyses, e.g., analyses for players, tactical groups, or for the entire team can be provided. Moreover, analyses for specific grids or critical areas (for example, the penalty box) concerning the

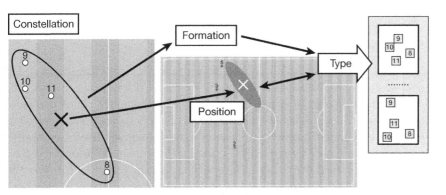

FIGURE 12.2 Net-based identification of formations and the regrouping with spatial and temporal information (Perl & Memmert, 2011)

Comparison: Bayern vs. Barca

Tactical Category	Game Opening <10m	Game Opening between 10–30m	Game Opening >30m	Sum
Bayern	65	46	8	119
Barca	119	97	8	224

Bayern Pass front = 61	D	M	O
Defense	9	8	0
Midfield	9	8	0
Offense	9	8	0

Bayern Pass back = 58	D	M	O
Defense	16	0	0
Midfield	6	29	0
Offense	0	2	5

Barca Pass front = 107	D	M	O
Defense	8	14	0
Midfield	0	64	5
Offense	0	0	20

Bayern Pass back = 117	D	M	O
Defense	13	0	0
Midfield	18	73	0
Offense	0	5	13

FIGURE 12.3 Passing movement statistics for FC Bayern Munich and FC Barcelona. The upper area shows all passes grouped by passing distance; the lower area shows passes forwards and backwards depending on the area of action

frequencies at each point in time and each period (for example, 1st/2nd halves, half-time) can be extracted.

Barcelona's Tiki-Taka becomes immediately apparent (Figure 12.3). Compared to Bayern Munich, they executed almost twice as many passes under 10 meters, and between 10 and 30 meters. Furthermore, they delivered almost twice as many passbacks, especially in the offensive zone.

Subsequently and based on this match, selected KPIs will be presented with a dynamic positional data analysis based on neuronal networks.

Interaction analysis

Positional data contain information on players' spatio-temporal formations on the field. Using the approach of neuronal networks, every neuron represents one type of such a formation and the cluster containing this neuron represents a collocation of this type. To use this method for the analysis of tactical processes in football, it is helpful to limit the formations to those of tactical groups like offense or defense, which are constituted by fewer players, and to hence separate them from their location on the field (Perl et al., 2013). In this way, the formation is reduced to just one temporal formation, whereas information concerning the position (the mean value of the players' positions for instance, also called "centroid") is stored separately for further analyses. The temporal series of these tactical formations depict the course of the game and allow for various kinds of process analysis. Two of these will briefly be introduced in subsequent examples.

The frequencies of the formations and their interactions can be measured and by this, they can provide information on which formations are preferred by which team and which tactical concepts are represented by these lineups (Grunz et al., 2012; Figures 12.4, 12.5).

Furthermore, tactical responses by, for example, the defense of a team to the offense activities of the other team can be analyzed and measured (Figure 12.6). If eventually the meaning of "success" is defined, the success of certain actions and interactions can be measured within the realm of formation—or a specific formation can be characterized if it is successful or not as shown below. In our case, the lineup of team A (FC Bayern Munich) is most successful when interacting with the defensive scheme against the most frequent lineups of team B (FC Barcelona) (Figure 12.7).

Let us return from the neural network approach to our Champions League match. Bayern started off well and got their first chance after just six minutes into the match. After another chance for Bayern, Barcelona got into the game and became stronger. What was striking was that Bayern were quite compact defensively, but the distance between center and full backs was too great (Figure 12.7). Their compact formation was also due to the minimal distance between the center backs and van Bommel. Zé Roberto played as a more offensive defensive midfielder, but was positioned too far from the back four and van Bommel. Thus, hardly any support for second balls was given and when overplayed, a large gap was created between center backs and midfielders.

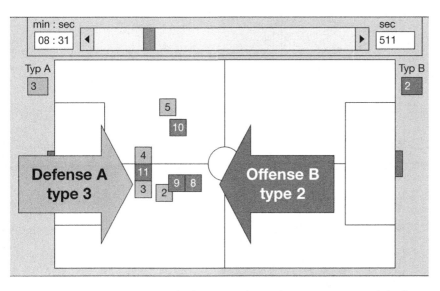

FIGURE 12.4 Two common tactical schemes in an actual game. Team A is defending, team B is attacking

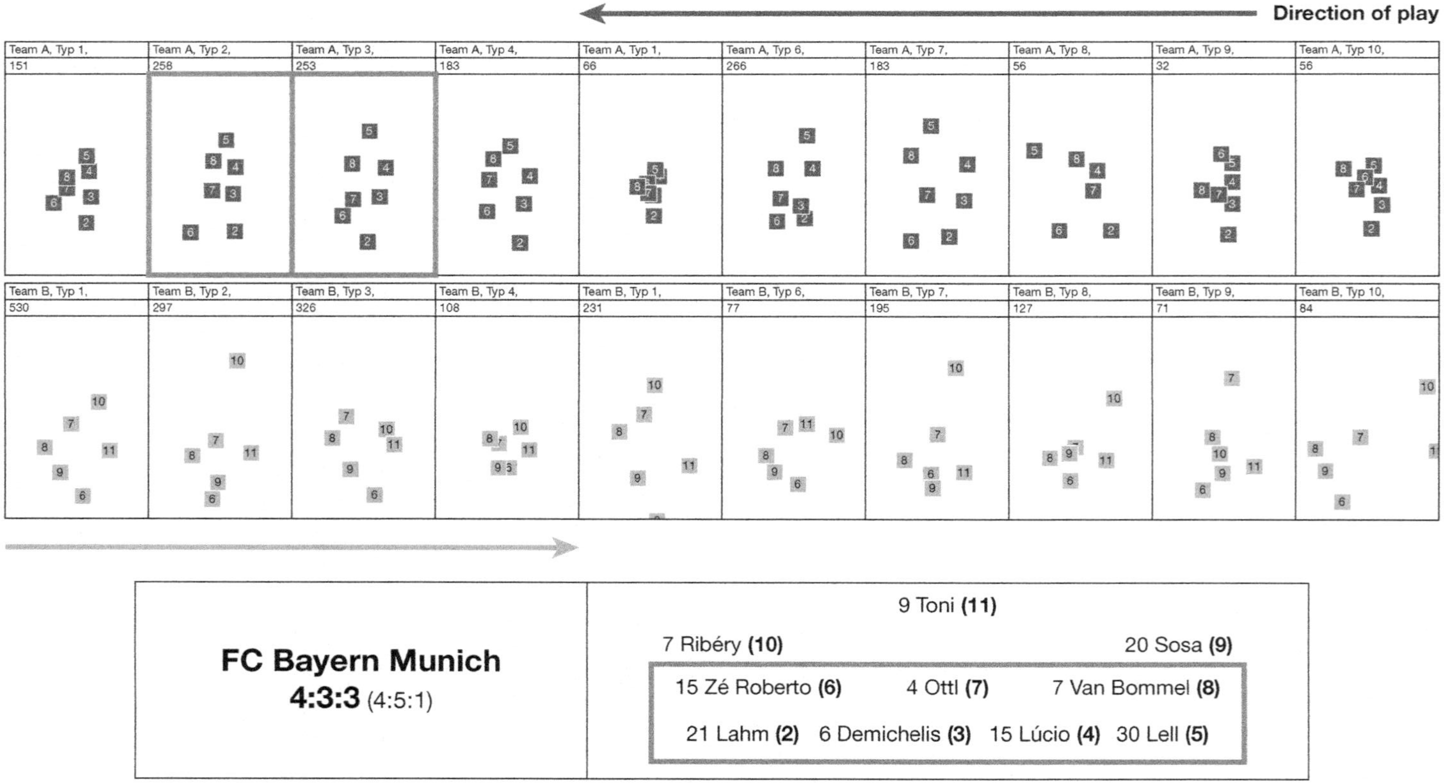

FIGURE 12.5 Tactical defense schemes frequently used by FC Bayern Munich (top) against the offensive schemes of FC Barcelona (bottom)

German	English translation
Team-bezogene Erfolgs-Analyse	Team related success analysis
Team-Auswahl	Team selection
erfolgreich	successful
Verteilungen im Formations-Kontext	Distributions in the formation context

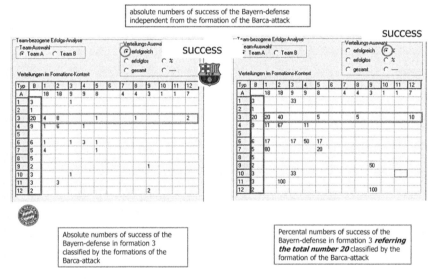

absolute numbers of success of the Bayern-defense
independent from the formation of the Barca-attack

Absolute numbers of success of the Bayern-defense in formation 3 classified by the formations of the Barca-attack

Percental numbers of success of the Bayern-defense in formation 3 *referring the total number 20* classified by the formation of the Barca-attack

FIGURE 12.6 Representation of the basic matrix of team success in the context of interaction

Another striking aspect according to the positional data of the first half was that the distance between the midfielder and center forward player, Toni was too far. Hence, he was left alone and didn't receive enough support when long balls were played (Figure 12.8). Ribéry (left midfield) played a little more in the offensive than Sosa on his side (right midfield). The entire defensive midfield, consisting of Zé Roberto, Van Bommel, and Ottl, was almost consistently lined up linearly, which made space partitioning impossible. A central player in the offensive midfield was often lacking, which created a missing link between defensive and offensive, as well as between right and left wings. Ribéry tried to cover the central gap, but played too often as a right winger.

In the second half, Ribéry scored, giving Bayern a deserved 1–0 lead. He played even more offensively minded and either hand-pushed through to the central offensive position behind Toni or acted as a second attacker next to him, offering him more support (Figure 12.10). However, the distances to the attackers were still too far, as the midfield pushed up too late so that Ribéry and Toni could not combine. Bayern Munich's lead, however, didn't destabilize Barcelona and Seydou Keita scored the equalizer after neat combination play.

German	English translation
Team-bezogene Erfolgs-Analyse	Team related success analysis
Team-Auswahl	Team selection
erfolgreich	successful
Verteilungen im Formations-Kontext	Distributions in the formation context

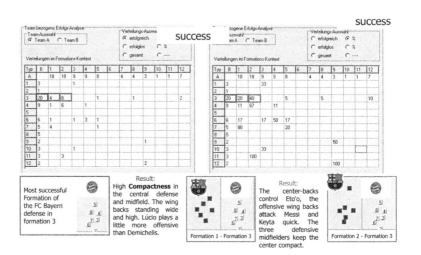

FIGURE 12.7 Team success in the context of interaction: Focus on Bayern Munich: 1st half—Team A, Bayern, attacks; Team B, Barcelona, defends. Distribution: 59 successful formations of which 20 A3 (33.9 per cent) were successful.

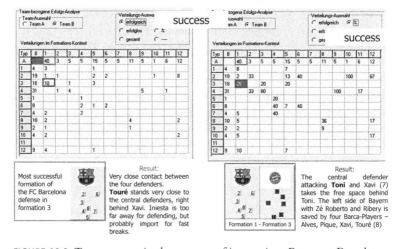

FIGURE 12.8 Team success in the context of interaction: Focus on Barcelona: 1st half—Team A, Bayern, attacks; Team B, Barcelona, defends. Distribution: 113 successful formations of which 40 B3 (35.4 per cent) were successful.

Direction of play

FIGURE 12.9 In the first half, it is noted which tactical offense schemes (top) Bayern Munich often used against which tactical defense schemes (bottom) of Barcelona.

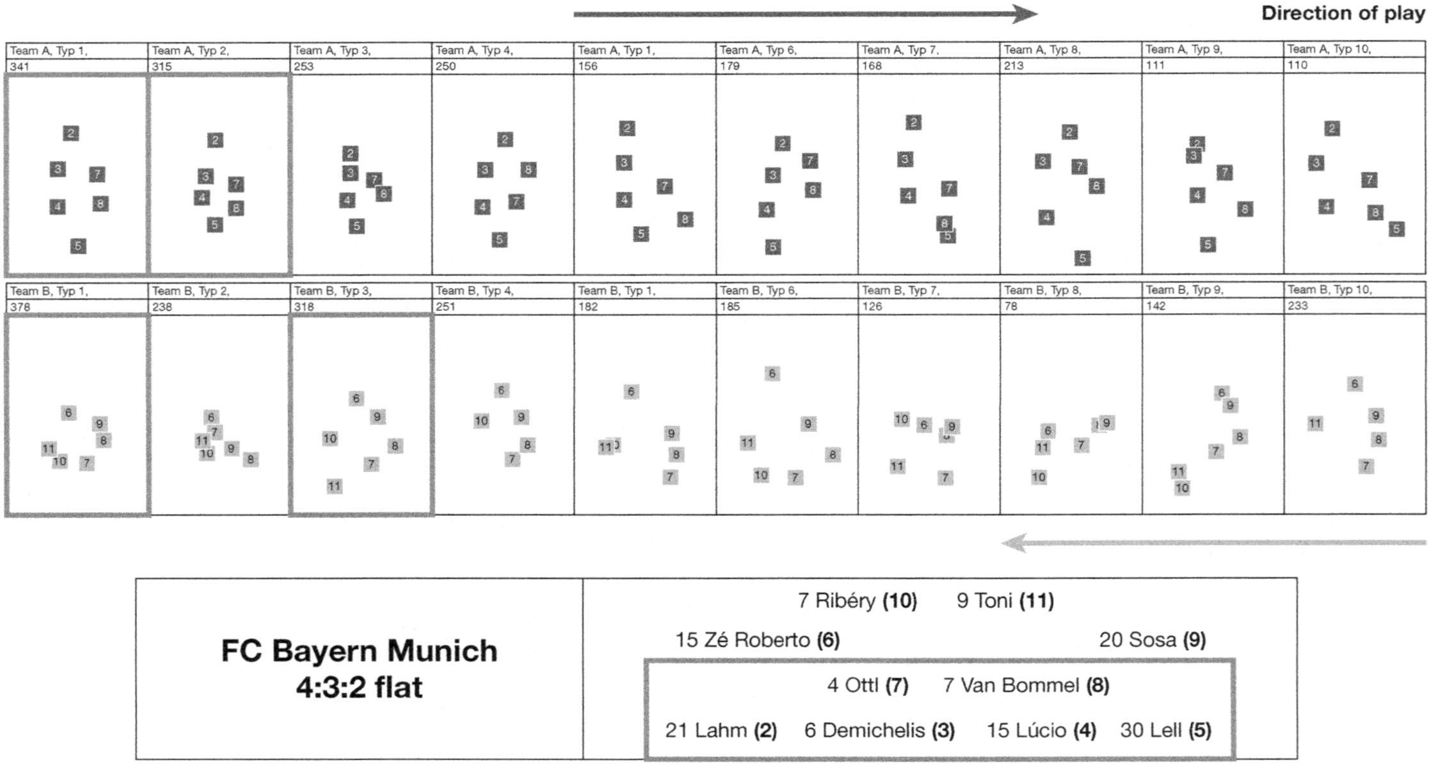

Direction of play

| Team A, Typ 1, 341 | Team A, Typ 2, 315 | Team A, Typ 3, 253 | Team A, Typ 4, 250 | Team A, Typ 1, 156 | Team A, Typ 6, 179 | Team A, Typ 7, 168 | Team A, Typ 8, 213 | Team A, Typ 9, 111 | Team A, Typ 10, 110 |

| Team B, Typ 1, 378 | Team B, Typ 2, 238 | Team B, Typ 3, 318 | Team B, Typ 4, 251 | Team B, Typ 1, 182 | Team B, Typ 6, 185 | Team B, Typ 7, 126 | Team B, Typ 8, 78 | Team B, Typ 9, 142 | Team B, Typ 10, 233 |

FC Bayern Munich
4:3:2 flat

15 Zé Roberto (6)   7 Ribéry (10)   9 Toni (11)   20 Sosa (9)

21 Lahm (2)   6 Demichelis (3)   4 Ottl (7)   7 Van Bommel (8)

15 Lúcio (4)   30 Lell (5)

FIGURE 12.10 In the second half it can be determined which tactical defense schemes (top) Bayern Munich often uses against which tactical offense schemes (bottom) of Barcelona.

Direction of play

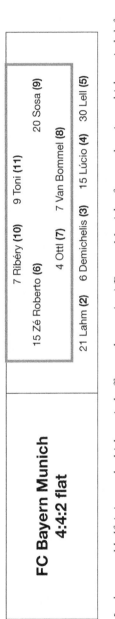

| Team A, Typ 1, 180 | Team A, Typ 2, 225 | Team A, Typ 3, 180 | Team A, Typ 4, 149 | Team A, Typ 1, 240 | Team A, Typ 6, 124 | Team A, Typ 7, 15 | Team A, Typ 8, 103 | Team A, Typ 9, 173 | Team A, Typ 10, 51 |

| Team B, Typ 1, 518 | Team B, Typ 2, 186 | Team B, Typ 3, 89 | Team B, Typ 4, 281 | Team B, Typ 1, 219 | Team B, Typ 6, 98 | Team B, Typ 7, 214 | Team B, Typ 8, 170 | Team B, Typ 9, 119 | Team B, Typ 10, 190 |

FC Bayern Munich
4:4:2 flat

7 Ribéry **(10)**   9 Toni **(11)**

15 Zé Roberto **(6)**   20 Sosa **(9)**

4 Ottl **(7)**   7 Van Bommel **(8)**

21 Lahm **(2)**   6 Demichelis **(3)**   15 Lúcio **(4)**   30 Lell **(5)**

FIGURE 12.11 In the second half, it is noted which tactical offense schemes (top) Bayern Munich often used against which tactical defense schemes (bottom) of Barcelona.

During half-time, the positional data revealed immediately what had to be changed to increase the chances of victory. According to the patterns in Figure 12.6, it became clear that Bayern positioned themselves much more widely in the second half and thus allowed the opposition more space. This happened at the expense of compactness. Barcelona scored a simple equalizer. Bayern changed their tactical formation from 4–5–1 to 4–4–2, in which Zé Roberto was now playing in the left midfield position previously filled by Ribéry. But in the offense, Bayern could have used an offensive midfielder (for example 4–3–2–1), as the distance between Toni and the defensive midfielders was too great. A player that helped secure high balls for Toni would have been necessary. A 4–3–2–1 system would have thus been the obvious option.

In the defense, Demichelis and Lúcio now played more in line. The defensive midfield continued in a compact formation, but the distance to the back four was too great leading to a higher risk against the ball. Both full backs, Lahm and Lell, were standing in much wider positions, whereas the former was standing more on the left side than the latter was on the right. In the second half Ribéry supported Toni more in the offense. He played without any restrictions, meaning that he changed from left to right as a center forward.

But the distances remained too great. Ottl and van Bommel remained in a very compact formation, but without any offensive action. The distance between Toni and the midfielders was again too great. Klinsmann didn't take any action against this. Zé Roberto and Sosa played a little higher up the field, which resulted in the goal. From a defensive perspective, a 4–3–3 against the ball would have been a good system against Barcelona, as the three defensive midfielders could have closed the center against the center attacks.

The pressing index

As shown in Chapter 11, the pressing index of a team or of players can be measured using a dynamic process analysis. This overall team value (in m/s) shows how fast all players move towards the ball to regain possession. Astonishingly, and in contrast to press reports, both teams acted nearly equally well against the ball (Figure 12.12).

What can be said about individual player pressing speeds? For instance, Luca Toni had the lowest value in the first half, whereas other Bayern players' speeds remained somewhat average. Based on the individual values of all players and average speed, parameters on the pressing performance strategy of the defensive team can be calculated. No significant difference between FC Bayern Munich (M = 4.5 m/s) and FC Barcelona (M = 4.3 m/s) was found. In the second half Luca Toni had the lowest values, whereas the others remained relatively steady. Ribéry achieved good values.

In conclusion, based on these patterns it can be seen that Bayern were lined up in a very compact way in the defensive center, but left too great a distance between the center backs (Demichelis, Lúcio) and the full backs (Lahm, Lell). Ottl as a defensive midfielder played somewhat more defensively than Zé Roberto and Van Bommel. Lúcio stayed slightly behind, as a hanging center back. Altogether

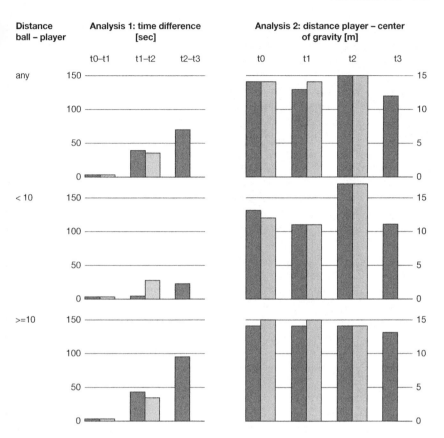

FIGURE 12.12 The pressing index of both teams in the different phases

the distance between the central defense and Ottl as defensive midfielder was very little, which resulted in good compactness. Zé Roberto as defensive midfielder played a more offensive role, but stood too far away from the back four, which meant that there was no possibility of him supporting second passes or balls. A large gap resulted when switching between attacking and defending.

Post-match analysis

After the match, automatic determination of real tactical formations during the game can be made based on positional data. Here it becomes clear that a well-known German sports magazine was not correct with its assumptions. The concluding analysis of the two coaches:

Jürgen Klinsmann (coach, FC Bayern Munich):

> Today we showed an excellent reaction to the prior defeat and gave a good account of ourselves against to absolute frontrunner on the title. Of course, we were dreaming of a miracle before the game and were hoping for an

FIGURE 12.13 Munich's Luca Toni looks disappointed after the equalizer (2009)

Source: John Macdougall/AFP/Getty Images

FC Bayern	1	2	3	4	5	6	7	8	9	10	11	Mean
Not in possession		17.1	12.9	13.0	15.8	11.7	5.8	7.5	15.2	15.9	17.5	13.2
In possession		24.2	20.7	20.0	18.4	19.5	15.4	16.1	18.0	20.4	24.6	19.7
Difference	0.0	-7.1	-7.8	-7.0	-2.7	-7.8	-9.6	-8.6	-2.8	-4.5	-7.1	-6.5
Diff. in %	0.0	-41.3	-60.9	-54	-16.9	-66.2	163.7	-115.0	-18.4	-28.3	-40.5	-49.0
FC Bayern	1	2	3	4	5	6	7	8	9	10	11	Mean
Not in possession		16.0	13.3	13.3	16.9	16.4	8.3	6.0	8.5	18.6	18.0	13.5
In possession		21.3	18.7	19.4	22.5	22.1	15.1	14.9	17.2	22.0	25.3	19.9
Difference	0.0%	-5.3	-5.4	-6.1	-5.7	-5.7	-6.9	8.9	-8.8	-3.4	-7.3	-6.3
Diff. in %	0.0%	-32.8	-40.6	-45.5	-33.8	-34.5	-82.9	-147.1	-103.9	-18.4	-40.3	-46.8

FIGURE 12.14 Individual pressing values of Munich and Barcelona players

early 1–0, which we would have needed with to upset Barcelona. Later, Ribéry was able to get the lead. If shortly after the penalty is awarded, it would be 2–0 and I'd love to see how the crowd gets going then. Of course, the game was decided when Barcelona got the equalizer. We've learned a lot from these two fixtures and we now know that we have to improve a lot of things for the UEFA Champions League next season. We had great ambitions, but ultimately failed because of a team that is a notch above.

Tito Vilanova (assistant coach, FC Barcelona):

We already knew that in this second leg it does not come down to having the ball at all times. Instead we had to have a tactically well and disciplined

UEFA Champions League, quarter final, second leg, 14.04.2009
FC Bayern Munich vs. FC Barcelona **1–1**

FIGURE 12.15 Line-up of FC Barcelona

UEFA Champions League, quarter final, second leg, 14.04.2009
FC Bayern Munich vs. FC Barcelona **1–1** (wrong lineup: *kicker*)

FIGURE 12.16 UEFA Champions League, quarter-final, FC Bayern Munich vs. FC Barcelona, wrong lineup FC Bayern

UEFA Champions League, quarter final, second leg, 14.04.2009
FC Bayern Munich vs. FC Barcelona **1-1** (actual lineup)

FIGURE 12.17 UEFA Champions League, quarter-final, FC Bayern Munich vs. FC Barcelona, correct lineup FC Bayern

positioning. It was clear that a goal for us would massively increase our position. However, we did not want to move forward with all our players on attack. Together with head coach Pep Guardiola we perfectly prepared for this match and we had planned which decisions were to be made, so that it was easy for me in my own responsibility. We are very glad to have come this far, now we are in the semifinals. But next we are concentrating on the league; Chelsea will come afterwards. Nevertheless, Chelsea is a strong opponent; after all, they were in the final last year.

This match shows that the series of formation types offers much information on the dynamic interaction of the opposition's tactical grouping. Thereby, information on frequently occurring interaction patterns was made available for analysis. As we will see later, neuronal net approaches can also detect rare, but important and possibly creative, actions and interactions from positional data. Also, additional advanced KPIs, such as the pressing index, can help to identify slow ball regain processes as an indicator for significant weakness of a team or players next to the qualitative interaction analysis.

References

Grunz, A., Memmert, D., & Perl, J. (2009). Analysis and simulation of actions in games by means of special self-organizing maps. *International Journal of Computer Science in Sport, 8,* 22–36.

Grunz, A., Memmert, D., & Perl, J. (2012). Tactical pattern recognition in soccer games by means of special self-organizing maps. *Human Movement Science, 31,* 334–343.

Memmert, D., Bischof, J., Endler, S., Grunz, A., Schmid, M., Schmidt, A., & Perl, J. (2011). World-level analysis in top level football. Analysis and simulation of football specific group tactics by means of adaptive neural networks. In C. L. P. Hui (Ed.), *Artificial Neural Networks – Application* (3–12), InTech, Available from: www.intechopen.com/articles/show/title/world-level-analysis-in-top-level-football-analysis-and-simulation-of-football-specific-group-tactic.

Memmert, D. & Perl, J. (2006). Analysis of game creativity development by means of continuously learning neural networks. In E. F. Moritz & S. Haake (Eds.). *The Engineering of Sport 6, Vol. 3* (pp. 261–266). New York: Springer.

Memmert, D. & Perl, J. (2009a). Analysis and simulation of creativity learning by means of artificial neural networks. *Human Movement Science, 28,* 263–282.

Memmert, D. & Perl, J. (2009b). Game creativity analysis by means of neural networks. *Journal of Sport Science, 27,* 139–149.

Perl, J. & Memmert, D. (2011). Net-based game analysis by means of the software tool SOCCER. *International Journal of Computer Science in Sport, 10,* 77–84.

Perl, J. & Memmert, D. (2012). Special issue: Network approaches in complex environments. *Human Movement Science, 31* (2), 267–270.

Perl, J., Grunz, A., & Memmert, D. (2013). Tactics in soccer: an advanced approach. *International Journal of Computer Science in Sport, 12,* 33–44. *Taktische Aufstellung von Bayern München und dem FC Barcelona im Champions League Viertelfinale 2008/09.* Veröffentlicht am 14. April 2009, von www.kicker.de/news/fussball/chleague/spielrunde/championsleague/2008-09/8/928060/taktische-austellung_bayern-muenchen-14_fc-barcelona.html

13

THE MYTH OF HOME ADVANTAGE

How Cologne fooled the statistics

After this excursion onto the international stage we now come back to the everyday life of the Bundesliga. For 1. FC Köln (Cologne), the first season after getting promoted back to the Bundesliga in 2014 was fairly satisfactory. During the 2014–2015 season the team was never in a relegation spot but mid-table, an achievement that can mostly be attributed to the solid defense and a strong keeper, Timo Horn. At the end of the season, the team was in 12th place and had played nine goalless draws, to set up a new Bundesliga record.

Looking more closely, one thing indeed does not really fit into the otherwise solid-looking season of the Cologne team: the major discrepancy between the performances at home and away. Focusing on the home and away table after 34 games played, the discrepancy could not have been wider. In the home table, only two goals away from relegation spot 16, the Cologne team would have finished fifth if only away games had counted, theoretically resulting in direct qualification for the Europe League. "Of course, we would like to change the record and win a lot of points at home. However, it does not matter where we get the points to avoid relegation. If we enter the history books by being the poorest home-team and the best outwards-team of the FC of all times, this is also okay for us," said coach Peter Stöger in February (Schmidt, 2015).

However, why didn't the Cologne team collect, as would any other team, their points at home? What happened to the supposed advantage of playing at home? Eventually this effect has been shown to exist exist in many sports, including top-level football, although of decreasing importance. Teams who perform in their own stadium and in front of their fans win on average more often than the visiting team; they gain more points and score more goals.

Despite the prominence of home advantage, the theory is not clearly proven. The explanation attempts on the other hand are manifold. Possible factors can be,

FIGURE 13.1 Timo Horn, goalkeeping for 1. FC Köln, saves the ball during a Bundesliga match against Hertha BSC at Olympiastadion (2015)

Source: Boris Streubel/Bongarts/Getty Images

on the one hand, the familiar environment as well as many cheering fans. On the other hand, the referee can also be the potential cause, as he may be unconsciously influenced by the atmosphere and thereby unintentionally gives decisions their way. Further, a kind of placebo effect is another theory by which the home team—merely by knowing they have an alleged home advantage—appears more offensive (Staufenbiel et al., 2015).

There is no place like home

For analysis of the cause of the puzzling results of 1. FC Köln, we must first investigate how the myth of home advantage translates to the advanced key performances indicators. It can be assumed that home teams are also favored in terms of outplayed opponents or spatial control. In comparison to the visiting team, they indeed prove to be better in several aspects. According to a study by Memmert et al. (2016) they outplayed the opposition, based on 50 Bundesliga games in the 2014–2015 season. Not only clearly more opposing players when passing into the offense, but can also control, while passing in midfield, with greater space in the offense and penalty areas. Further, while passing in the attacking zone, they won significantly more space in the opponents' penalty area.

Moreover, a more defensive orientation of the visiting team can be observed in general. The home team faces more opposing players in midfield if the ball is passed from the midfield towards or within the attacking zone. To sum up, also in measurements that go beyond fundamental performance parameters, a difference

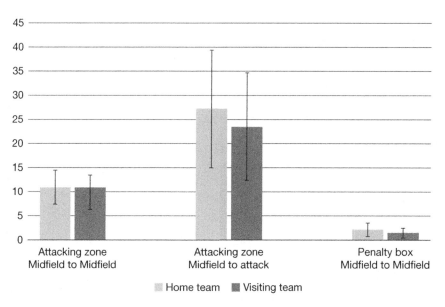

FIGURE 13.2 The home team clearly has more spatial control in the opponents' 30-meter zone and penalty box than the away team

in favor of the hosts can be measured. However, this advantage in one's own stadium is steadily decreasing.

On the basis of this information, the case of the so-called "Effzeh" can be solved. The performance of the Cologne team, comparing the games in the Rheinenergie Stadium and those away from home, partially show the same differences as the typical home advantage—with reversed signs!

Surprisingly, the Cologne team performed worse at home in the categories that should favor the home team—compared to the matches they played as the away team. Especially, passes in the attacking zone outplayed fewer opponents at home as away. What seems to be in general easier for home teams tends to be especially hard for the Cologne team. For the team headed by Peter Stöger, the season was nevertheless a success.

References

Schmidt, J. (February 4, 2015). Mit Masterplan gegen die Heimschwäche. *General Anzeiger Bonn.* Retrieved from www.general-anzeiger-bonn.de/sport/fckoeln/Mit-Masterplan-gegen-die-Heimschw%C3%A4che-article1553596.html

Staufenbiel, K., Lobinger, B., & Strauss, B. (2015). Home advantage in soccer—A matter of expectations, goal setting and tactical decisions of coaches? *Journal of Sports Science, 33,* 1932–1941.

14

MANAGERIAL INFLUENCE

Catapult seat in Palermo

For many people, being a football manager sounds like a dream job. What we sometimes forget is the fact that this job can be brutally hard. Coaches work around the clock, are permanently in the focus of the public, and are under enormous pressure. The tests come once or twice per week and thus makes this job as ephemeral as no other. And it seems to be irrelevant how well technically a coach does his job. In the end, almost exclusively the lack of success determines

FIGURE 14.1 "Cult coach" Thomas Schaaf: over 14 years in 644 games for Werder Bremen on the sidelines

a dismissal. It is a fine line between success and failure in a game, in which around half of all goals follow some kind of coincidence.

Studies show that changes in managerial position do not have any impact in the long run (Heuer et al., 2011; Memmert et al., 2013). Nevertheless, many football club boards of teams in a precarious situation tend to go for a change in coaching staff. Nowhere else in the 21st century has the trainer carousel turned more rapidly than for the Italian side US Palermo, which has experienced over 30 changes in the position of head coach in the past 14 years. But this does not have to be the case, as some examples from the Bundesliga show. For these, long-term development with the same coach counts for more than short-term reactions.

SV Werder Bremen is a prime example of this approach. Trainer Thomas Schaaf has supervised the team for more than 14 years, over 644 matches, and won the German Championship once and the cup three times. His retirement in May 2012 marked an end to an era and initiated a rebuilding phase at the Weser. The first season after Schaaf left, the club, now under Robin Dutt, finished in the lower half of the table. In the following season (2014–2015), the team was forced to act and Dutt was replaced by Viktor Skripnik.

Skripnik, a former player under Schaaf, managed to lead the struggling Bremen team to a solid 10th place, winning an average of 1.56 points per match. This was a good performance, almost resulting in qualification for the UEFA Europa League. From a tactical perspective, these two coaching periods have been shaped mainly by two different playing systems which, at first glimpse, seem to be quite similar. On further investigation, they serve as the ideal basis to investigate technical aspects of two different playing styles under two coaches.

Versions of 4–4–2

Under Dutt, Bremen played in a classical 4–4–2 formaton with two central defensive midfielders. Skripnik practiced a 4–4–2 system as well, but in a diamond formation consisting of an offensive as well as a defensive midfielder. Thomas Schaaf, who favored this system, had also made Bremen well known for their use of the diamond formation. It was a change in detail and was celebrated as a reintroduction of more traditional virtues.

The difference between both systems, 4–4–2 flat and 4–4–2 diamond, consisted not in the general positions but rather in the style of playing. In the system with defensive midfielders, the Werder team tried to play possession football with controlled buildup and organized attacks. Control was the keyword. Skripnik interpreted the style of the team a little bit differently and used the diamond to control space. The intention was to use the offensive midfielders to gain better in-depth control in midfield. The two central midfielders were not positioned on the same line and a double occupation of the space before the defense was therefore no longer possible.

Comparing the results of four games of Werder Bremen under Dutt with corresponding rematches under Skripnik, the data confirm this theory. The additiona offensive midfield player helped to control more space in critical zones. The team was able to control roughly 30 per cent more space in the attacking zone when playing passes from the midfield into this zone after switching to the diamond formation. In the penalty area, they even recorded a rate of about 70 per cent. On average, control increased from 18.44 to 24.09 per cent in the attacking zone and from 4.52 to 7.83 per cent in the penalty area.

Even though more spatial control was achieved, Bremen under Skripnik did not play the same ball possession football as with Dutt. Rather the additional

10th match day, Sat. (01.11.14) 1. FSV Mainz 05 vs. SV Werder Bremen, (4–2–3–1) **1–2** (4–4–2 diamond) *Coach V. Skripnik*

FIGURE 14.2 FSV Mainz 05 vs. SV Werder Bremen, showing Bremen's 4–4–2 diamond formation

player in the offensive center was utilized to play fast and steep vertical passes. With the new option up front and wingers moving up quickly, Werder were able to initiate fast counterattacks after gaining possession. With a faster bypassing of midfield and more offensive-minded players when in attack, they managed to generate much more space.

As indicated in Table 14.1, for all passes in the offensie area, i.e., from the midfield into and within the attacking zone, greater space gains were achieved on average in both critical zones when Skripnik was head coach.

7th match day, Sat. (04.10.14) SV Werder Bremen vs. SC Freiburg, (4–4–2 double 6) **1–1** (4–4–2 double 6) *Coach R. Dutt*

FIGURE 14.3 SV Werder Bremen vs. SC Freiburg, showing Bremen's 4–4–2 flat formation

TABLE 14.1 Average spatial gain by the Bremen team in the four matches of the first and second legs

		4–4–2 flat	4–4–2 diamond
Passes into the attacking zone	Space gain, attacking zone	2.80	3.45
	Space gain, penalty area	0.66	2.81
Passes within the attacking zone	Space gain. attacking zone	0.83	2.43
	Space gain, penalty area	1.44	3.95

It is not too surprising that spatial control increases in the attacking zone when utilizing an additional offensive player. However, it is clear that tactical changes under Skripnik resulted in the intended improvements in terms of spatial control and gains. The idea of relinquishing match control to gain more open spaces for counterattacking worked. The comparison furthermore outlines how changing the manager can lead to measureable differences in tactical performance.

References

Heuer, A., Müller, C., Rubner, O., Hagemann, N., & Strauss, B. (2011). Usefulness of dismissing and changing the coach in professional soccer. *PLoS ONE 6*: e17664. doi:10.1371/journal.pone.0017664

Memmert, D., Strauß, B., & Theweleit, D. (2013). *Der Fußball—Die Wahrheit*. Münchn: Süddeutsche Zeitung Edition.

15
ALL ON ATTACK

Variability pays off

"If you are behind, you have to bring a defender." This statement, by the legendary Johan Cruyff, may seem odd and certainly does not match everyone's intuition. Shouldn't we expect the introduction of another striker as being the best strategy to deal with being behind?

FIGURE 15.1 Peter Stöger, head coach of 1. FC Köln (2015)

The team 1. FC Köln, under tactical direction of Peter Stöger, shows that adding an extra offensive player does not automatically lead to dominance in offense. We have already observed the defensive stability and regularly poor home performances in the 2014–2015 season. Let's have a look at another component of their convincing performances in the season discussed in a previous chapter: tactical variability.

1st match day, Sat. (23.08.14). 1. FC Köln vs. Hamburger SV, (4–2–3–1) **0–0** (4–2–3–1)	space control: 12.03 % – Cologne's space control inside the box when passing in the attacking zone	1–3 % – Cologne's passes within or between midfield and attacking zone

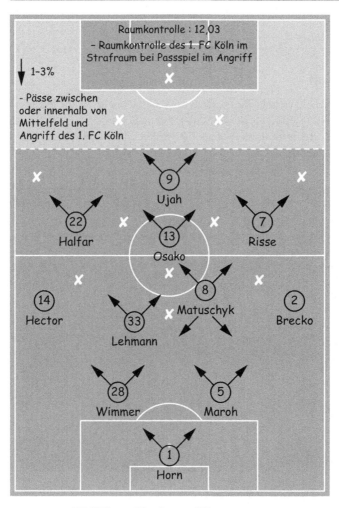

FIGURE 15.2 FC Köln vs. Hamburger SV

Throughout the second half of the season, 4–4–2 emerged as the favored system although the team previously proved that they could switch among a broad range of systems. They not only played the common 4–2–3–1 system but also could switch to a back five if needed. The team was capable of adapting their system to their opponents', and not only before kick-off. Even during the match, they were willing to react and adapt to changes in the scoreline or their opponents' tactics.

4th match day, Sat. (21.09.14). 1. FC Köln vs. Borussia M'Gladbach, (4–4–2) **0–0** (4–4–2)	space control: 6.80 % - Cologne's space control inside the box when passing in the attacking zone	1–3 % - Cologne's passes within or between midfield and attacking zone

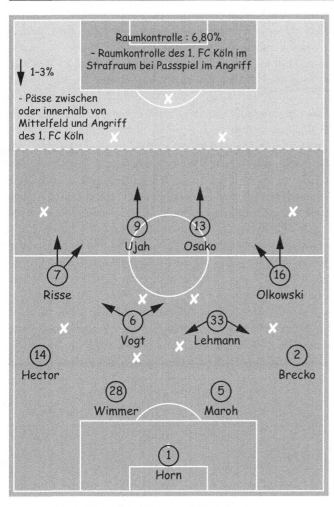

FIGURE 15.3 1. FC Köln vs. Borussia M'Gladbach

The above-mentioned 4–2–3–1, a system with five midfielders, was particularly common with Cologne when facing allegedly weaker opponents. By changing to five midfielders they were able to provide more passing opportunities in the center, improving their game control. Against top teams they instead focused on a compact defense and counterattacking, but when playing against a lesser opponent they tried to use an additional midfielder to avoid the other team imposing their own strategy.

System and playing style

But how does a missing striker affect the spatial control metrics? Does the team lose offensive effectiveness and power by overcrowding the midfield? Comparing the two systems reveals that Cologne indeed has had more space dominance up front when playing with an additional midfielder. In their 4–2–3–1 system, on average they controlled one to three percentage points more space than usual in the attacking zone. Similar effects were observable in the opponent's penalty area—but with one small but important exception: If they played the ball within attack they were able to control almost twice as much space as usual (12.03 rather than 6.80 per cent).

Interpretation of these performance data must consider the system as well as the playing style. When Cologne played in a 4–4–2 formation there were usually fewer players moving up during attack. This defensively oriented style often left strikers on their own while other players were trying to supply them with long balls. On the other hand, if they wished to control the opposition using their 4–2–3–1 system, the midfielders stepped in and helped in the attack. Although missing one striker, there were more players involved in structured attacking in total and they were even able to dominate more space in the critical zones.

However, the system was chosen only when Stöger trusted his squad to stay in possession without losing defensive stability against the other team, as this offensive way of playing comes with more players up front and can easily cause problems when facing more organized opponents.

Therefore, playing with two forwards is only superficially the more offensive variation compared using to a single striker. Taking the interpretation of a system and its style into account, the latter option can lead to more pressure in offense. How an extra defender could benefit the offense, like Cruyff suggested, has yet to be discovered.

16
LAWS OF A DERBY

Special rivalries

Whether Old Firm or Superclásico, derbies are special, although it has not yet been scientifically proved that they follow their own rules as is often claimed. But this is only a minor factor in this case. Regarding emotion, drama, and meaning, they are in a league of their own. Thus, it had to be a derby that we chose for the subsequent analysis.

So far, we have seen from several examples how positional data cast a new light on tactical aspects in football at all levels. From macroscopic investigations about

FIGURE 16.1 Hakan Çalhanoğlu scores the second goal with a direct free kick during the derby match between Bayer 04 Leverkusen and 1. FC Köln (2014)

Source: Patrik Stollarz/AFP/Getty Images

Bayer 04 Leverkusen 5–1 (1–1) 1. FC Köln
Saturday 29 November, 2014—15:30
Match day 13, 2014–2015 Season

BayArena, Leverkusen

0–1 Lehmann (4th minute)
1–1 Bellarabi (26th)
2–1 Calhanoglu (61st)
3–1 Drmic (79th)
4–1 Drmic (88th)
5–1 Bellarabi (90th)

victory or defeat, detailed insights on tactics and system changes, to live analyses during matches. Now, we will focus again on a single match and examine the follow-up analysis.

How will the match report of the future look like? To this day, post-match analyses are done mostly by hand. Indeed, it these are produced intensively with video recordings, and comprehensive statistics are also gathered. However, the subjectivity of the reports predominates. The subsequent example will illustrate, similarly to the Champions League semi-final between Bayern Munich and Barcelona from a previous chapter, how such a manually conducted match analysis can be complemented by the selective use of key performance indicators based on positional data. The Rhenish derby between Bayer 04 Leverkusen and 1. FC Köln on the 13th match day of the 2014–2015 campaign, which was won 5–1 by Bayer Leverkusen, serves as our test object.

Summary of the course of the game

From the start of the game, Cologne especially focused on the defensive aspect. Therefore, the early lead following Lehmann's penalty played into the visitors' hands. Long balls to Ujah remained the mean of choice for attacking, however, few players supported the strikers on the rare counterattacks. Leverkusen, in contrast, were completely in control of the match for most of the time but had little chance against Cologne's compact defensive setup from the beginning. It had to be a set-piece that led to the equalizer in the middle of the first half, when Bellarabi punished Horn's goalkeeping mistake. Fifteen minutes after the break, once again a free-kick lead to a breakthrough when Calhanoglu scored directly. Cologne subsequently shifted to a 4–4–2, and coach Peter Stöger brought on two new attackers, Osako and Finne. At this point the match became much more open, but still Cologne seldom threatened Leno's goal. Instead, the space now emerging invited Leverkusen to counterattack. Two counterattacking goals, from Drmic and Bellarabi, ensured a decisive win for Leverkusen.

Formation and lineup

Cologne's focus on the defense could already be guessed in view of the starting lineup. The team operated in a 5–4–1, where Maroh played next to Wimmer and Mavraj in the defensive center, the wingbacks Hector and Brecko completing the back five. The midfield was formed by Lehmann and Vogt in the center, with Svento and Olkowski playing as left and right midfielders. Ujah performed as the sole striker.

Leverkusen, on the other hand, played a 4–2–3–1. Boenisch, Spahic, Jedvaj, and Hilbert defended in the back four, with two offensively minded wingbacks. Castro and Bender were positioned in the defensive midfield before them, the offensive midfield being composed of Son, Calhanoglu, and Bellarabi, whereas both the offensive left and right midfield players were well forward, positioning themselves just short of the main striker, Kießling.

Defensive order and the transition game

Cologne's formation did not change when the ball was with the opposition. They defended with all players very deep in the own half (defensive pressing). The lone striker Ujah positioned himself as first defender at the level of the halfway line or even on the center circle. Thus Leverkusen was given the opportunity to realize their game plan. Only when they tried to pass the ball to their own striker or to play through central midfield did the Cologne players start to defend.

The outer longitudinal zones of the pitch were defended somewhat collaterally, so that Bayer frequently tried to play on the flanks. Cologne kept their lines close together and as a result minimized the space for passes. The defensive row were positioned mostly level with the penalty box, resulting in a compact central area. Especially after loss of possession, Cologne tried to drop back into their own half, regrouping as fast as possible to enable collective defending.

Leverkusen stuck to their basic plan when not in possession. The team around manager Roger Schmidt defended very offensively, though: They positioned themselves about 10–15 meters into the opponent's half during organized buildups and tried to disrupt or even prevent these directly. With this offensive pressing, the most offensive defending strategy, they attacked the opposition in their own half of the pitch and put early pressure on them. But they frequently left too large gaps between their lines as not all their players moved quickly enough out of defense. After losing possession, Leverkusen attempted to disrupt the opposition's counterattacking by direct counter-pressing, aiming to regain possession immediately. When this succeeded, the players regrouped in their original formation. When in possession, the center backs Spahic and Jedvaj positioned themselves very high up the pitch, favored by their deep-lying opponents, and repeatedly progressed to the halfway line.

Attacking play

Regarding the buildup and actual game, Cologne trusted in long balls to the lone striker Ujah most of the time. To evade Leverkusen's counter-pressing during the build-up, the visitors tried to outfox the opposition with vertical balls. The data show a range of passes to striker Ujah that bypassed more than four opponents. The first of these took out five Leverkusen players after just 18 seconds. It was Ujah's task to secure these balls or to try to outpace the markers.

The focus on counterattacking becomes obvious when looking at the passing data collected. In both halves, Cologne were opposed by only half as many Leverkusen players as their opponents. Additionally, Cologne gained 6.5 (1st half) and 5.6 (2nd half) percentage points of space with passes to their forwards in the attacking zone, whereas Leverkusen could only manage 0.6 and 0.05 percentage points, respectively. Because of the offensive positioning of Leverkusen, the Cologne defenders on average outplayed half an opponent more during the opening period.

On the other hand, Leverkusen had a variety of options and were troubled little. Because of Cologne's very compact defensive setup, Leverkusen attempted to spread the game to the wings in the first part of the pitch. Therefore, the wingbacks positioned themselves relatively high up and tried to dribble the ball into the opposition's half before passing infield. Passes were delayed, Boenisch and Hilbert played aggressively often waiting until there was direct contact with an opponent. The subsequent vertical game was rather ineffective.

Another ploy to open up the Cologne defense became obvious during the course of the match: initiating the buildup in the center with long, uncontrolled balls to the frontmen. Castro often fell back between the two center backs to regain possession of the ball, or Spahic as a center back played wide passes into the Cologne defense. Leverkusen partially succeeded in bridging the midfield and generally outplaying the Cologne defense. Solid pressing and quick counterattacks helped Leverkusen to create space and good scoring opportunities. Especially in the final quarter, a few more promising counterattacks were possible thanks to Cologne's more offensive tactics.

Leverkusen's superiority was especially noted in terms of possession in the first half. In terms of possession in the final third, 21.68 per cent and 21.82 per cent for the first and second halves was recorded. In contrast, the figures for Cologne with their rare goal attempts were only could claim only 10.26 and 11.28, respectively. The difference between passes during the final third was especially great in the opposition penalty area: Leverkusen 11.09 per cent and Cologne 1.61 per cent, respectively.

Cologne's change of system

Cologne's change of system came with a personnel switch in the 69th minute. Peter Stöger brought on Osako for Brecko, reorganizing the defense to a back four and adding another striker. In the new 4–4–2, Osako took on the role of a defensive forward. After Cologne's defensive tactics had been proved to be successful for most of the game, the coach had to act to try to grab at least one point.

And indeed, Cologne's performance data testify to a distinctly more attacking style in the second half: Control in with passes in the final third increased from an average of 13.74 per cent to 55.56 per cent. Instead of long balls up to the front, Cologne tried to employ a passing game.

This tactical change, together with Cologne's distinctly more offensive performance after falling behind, is also observable in Leverkusen's performance data. Although Leverkusen managed to exercise a similar amount of control in both

13th match day, Sat. (29.11.2014), Bayer 04 Leverkusen vs. 1. FC Köln, (4–2–3–1) **5–1** (5–4–1)

FIGURE 16.2 Cologne's setup until the 69th minute

13th match day, Sat. (29.11.2014), Bayer 04 Leverkusen vs. 1. FC Köln, (4–2–3–1) **5–1** (4–4–2)

FIGURE 16.3 Cologne's setup after the 69th minute

halves, much more space was created in the second half by Cologne's tactical change. Leverkusen increased their possession in the final third from 33.09 to 48.09 per cent and from 11.09 to 29.02 per cent in the penalty box.

Individual player performances

To give an analysis on the performance of individual players, at this point we will look at—also regarding the tactical setup—the average outplayed positions as well as *pressure efficiency*.

Pressure efficiency is an extension of the indicator for outplayed players, which is especially useful in the evaluation of individual performances. To measure this, all passes by a player that outplay at least one opponent are weighted—on the one hand with the pressure that the closest opponent puts on the passer, on the other with the space that the pass receiver has at his/her disposal after receiving the ball. This figure therefore models a player's ability to play efficient offensive passes under pressure. For a detailed examination, please see Chapter 17.

In the first half, the rapid bridging of the midfield had a particular impact on the performance data of the visiting team. With long balls out of defense, the midfield players were relatively ineffective. In addition, due to Leverkusen putting considerable pressure on the Cologne defenders, better ratings were recorded. Hector and Wimmer rated particularly high, the latter recording the top values concerning pressure efficiency (4.24) and outplaying two opponents with his passes on average. By comparison, Svento was bottom of the list with a pressure efficiency of 0.43, and −1 outplayed positions (position losses).

In the second half, the previously high values for the Cologne defender declined. Only Maroh (pressure efficiency 3.76) and Olkowski (outplayed 2.5 opponents on average) stand out, a sign that the most effective moves were on the right-hand side. But altogether—the midfielders' ratings were comparatively low—Cologne were rarely able to threaten the Leverkusen goal.

Compared to their opposition, Leverkusen were convincing with very high rating for pressure efficiency. Spahic recorded the top value in the second half (5.9), and the team on average were more efficient in their forward play forward. In particular, both wingbacks outplayed more opponents than more central players.

Facing a team defending compactly, Leverkusen had difficulty create chances for long periods. They tried again and again to play down the wings in the attacking third of the pitch and to circumvent the congested center. The next highest pressure efficiency is attributed to Boenisch, with on average 1.0 and 1.8 outplayed opponents per pass in the first and second halves, respectively. Also Hilbert outplayed on average 0.85 Cologne players with his passes in the first half. In contrast, the team's mean score was 0.22.

Three selected situations

1. Especially in the final quarter of the game, Leverkusen were consistently invited to counterattack. A good exasmple of this was in the 84th minute, when one of Horn's goalkicks was intercepted in his own half (Figure 16.4). Castro then managed to outplay six opponents. With an additional gain of 10 percentage points of space in the attacking zone, that pass resulted in a promising 2-on-2 situation.

FIGURE 16.4 Game situation 1

Source: © DFL—Deutsche Fußball Liga GmbH

2. An effective method used by Leverkusen to penetrate Cologne's defensive fortress was their use of one-twos, in which the initiating player bursts into free space to receive the ball again (Figure 16.5). One such instance happened in the 35th minute: After a throw-in, Bender passed the ball out to the wing, already taking one opponent out of play with this pass into the space. With this relatively simple pass to Son, Bayer's players doubled their possession in the attacking zone with 10.3 percentage points, to a total of 20.8 per cent. Bender also drew opponents out of their zone with this tactic and thus created space which Son was then able to use. Son, in the attacking zone, then had enough time to control the ball and burst toward the goal. Subsequently, Cologne tried to close down the ball carrier and, in doing so, won back four percentage points of control in the final third.

Yet, by moving up, Leverkusen gained space in the penalty area (1.1 percentage points). Son then played a one-two with Bellarabi with an interesting effect: While the first pass outplayed three opponents although without gaining space, exactly the opposite happened when Bellarabi passed back. The comparatively short return pass outplayed no further opponents but gained Leverkusen considerable possession, specifically 5.8 percentage points in the attacking third and 3.7 percentage points in the penalty area.

Therefore, they succeeded in cracking one defensive line with the first, releasing pass. After that, Son moved off the ball in a manner opening space in front of him when receiving the ball, subsequently entering the penalty area. Particularly crucial was the timing, which was perfect with Bellarabi's short pass.

3. A situation from the 53rd minute shows the consequences of a long, horizontal pass. Spahic, about 10 meters into the opposing half, lured Cologne's first defensive row out of position with a poor pass. Nevertheless, he subsequently

managed to pass the ball to Lars Bender, positioned 15 meters further to the right. With this movement of the Cologne midfield out of position, a wide space between defense and offense was created, containing all three of Leverkusen's offensive midfield players (Figure 16.6). The control rating in the attacking zone thus increased from 14.6 to 22.3 per cent with this pass.

There was also a change in the box. Due to the small sideways shift and Cologne's out-shifting in midfield, the defensive chain found itself constrained to orientate accordingly. It moved out to keep the distance between the rows as small as possible, pushing them to Bender's side. As a result, free space for Drmic was

FIGURE 16.5A AND B Game situation 2

Source: © DFL—Deutsche Fußball Liga GmbH

FIGURE 16.6 Game situation 3

Source: © DFL—Deutsche Fußball Liga GmbH

created behind the defense, which extended just into the penalty area. For a brief moment, Leverkusen controlled 11.9 per cent of the penalty area as opposed to 0.2 per cent prior to that pass. Leverkusen subsequently moved their attack further over toward the right wing and the Cologne defense managed to close the gaps again. The free space for Drmic and Boenisch on the left wing would have been effective passing options for Bender—although associated with a greater risk.

17

WHO WILL BE NOMINATED FOR THE FIFA WORLD CUP 2018?

The agony of choice

In May 2018, Jogi Löw, head coach of the German national team, will announce his squad for the FIFA World Cup in Russia. By then he and his coaching staff will have seen many Bundesliga and Champions League matches and they have got their impressions of potential players. He will also have access to physiological data, like sprints or running performances and qualitative information from his scouts and match analysts by the team led by Urs Siegenthaler, Christofer Clemens, and Dr. Stephan Nopp. And he will study this information extensively. Only then, maybe in consultation with his sports psychologist, Dr. Hans-Dieter Herrmann, will he decide and announce their decision to the general public.

The previous chapters have presented new KPIs, based on positional data that can be evaluated in seconds, providing another possibility for individual evaluation of individual performances. This was suggested in the previous chapters and shall now be further developed. Therefore, the football player becomes utterly transparent, and their performances on the pitch can be measured and recognized.

In the following, we will have another look at the KPI outplayed position, which we have already presented and discussed in Chapters 10 and 16. When this is expanded, as in Chapter 16, it can create a quality feature for successful passes and we can relate to it as *pressure efficiency* in the passing game.

Pressure efficiency measures how efficiently a player can outplay opponents while under pressure and how much space the ball receiver has when controlling the ball. Three components influence the calculation: the number of outplayed opponents, pressure by the nearest opponent on the passing player, and pressure on the pass receiver. The average of all passes is considered in which at least one player was outplayed. The higher the coefficient, the more efficient and better is the passing game (Rein, Raabe, & Memmert, 2017).

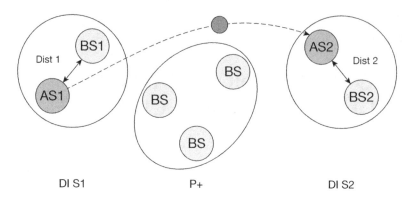

DI S1   P+   DI S2

FIGURE 17.1
Calculation of pressure efficiency according to the formula PEff = P+ × sqrt(Dist 2/ Dist 1). AS and BS are players in teams A and B, respectively; AS1, pressured by BS1 (closest opponent to AS1), plays a pass to AS2 who is being pressured by BS2 (closest opponent to AS2). Dist 1/DIS 1 is the distance between AS1 and BS1; Dist 2/DIS2 is the distance between AS2 and BS2; P+ is the "number of outplayed opponents," i.e., the players that are positioned between AS1 and AS2 when the pass is played and are therefore taken out of the game by this pass

Which full-back will get nominated for the FIFA World Cup?

FIGURE 17.2A Jonas Hector
Source: © Stuart Franklin/Bongarts/Getty Images

FIGURE 17.2B Matthias Ginter
Source: © Boris Streubel/Getty Images

TABLE 17.1 Hector and Ginter

Type of data	Pressure efficiency	
Full back	Jonas Hector	Matthias Ginter
1. HT	3.04	1.88
2. HT	1.7	1.71

Which center back will get nominated for the FIFA World Cup?

FIGURE 17.3A Mats Hummels
Source: © VI Images via Getty Images)

FIGURE 17.3B Jérôme Boateng
Source: © VI Images via Getty Images

TABLE 17.2 Hummels and Boateng

Type of data	Pressure efficiency	
Center back	Mats Hummels	Jérôme Boateng
1. HT	2.5	3.42
2. HT	1.15	1.73

Which defensive midfielder will get nominated for the FIFA World Cup?

FIGURE 17.4A Toni Kroos
Source: © Nolwenn Le Gouic/Icon Sport via Getty Images)

FIGURE 17.4B Ilkay Gündogan
Source: © Boris Streubel/Getty Images

TABLE 17.3 Kroos and Gündogan

Type of data	Pressure efficiency	
Def. midfield	Toni Kroos	Ilkay Gündogan
1. HT	3.25	2.66
2. HT	2.42	1.74

Which offensive midfielder will get nominated for the FIFA World Cup?

FIGURE 17.5A Marco Reus
© Matthias Hangst/Bongarts/Getty Images

FIGURE 17.5B Mesut Özil
Source: © Nolwenn Le Gouic/Icon Sport via Getty Images

FIGURE 17.5C Thomas Müller
Source: © VI Images via Getty Images

TABLE 17.4 Reus, Özil and Müller

Type of data	Pressure efficiency		
Off. midfield	Marco Reus	Mesut Özil	Thomas Müller
1. HT	0.94	1.43	4.57
2. HT	1.43	2.93	1.92

References

Rein, R., Raabe, D., & Memmert, D. (2017). "Which pass is better?" Novel approaches to assess passing effectiveness in elite soccer. *Human Movement Science*, *55*, 172–181.

18

CONCLUSION

A debate between possession and counterattacking playing styles

Do you remember the friendly match between Red Bull Salzburg and FC Bayern Munich at the Salzburg Red Bull arena on 18th January, 2014? At that time star coach Pep Guardiola encountered the largely unknown Salzburg coach Roger Schmidt. The match ended, rather surprisingly, 3–0 to the Austrians (Figure 18.1). Even though it was just a friendly, Guardiola later made memorable statements in an interview:

> The opponent was better than us. It was a lesson for us.
>
> *Süddeutsche Zeitung*, 2014

> It was a good lesson for the second half of the season. Salzburg played very well with and without the ball, congratulations. Many people have said to me during our training camp: "Bayern always wins anyway, Bayern, being such a big team, is just too good for all small teams." But we can lose, we have seen this today. So I am very pleased with this.
>
> *Focus Online*, 2014

> We have lost because of a different reason. We have a big squad, so it is normal that someone is injured. We have lost, because the opponent was better and because of my decisions. We wanted to try a back three instead of a back four today.
>
> *Focus Online*, 2014

This match, in which the team from Munich had their usual ball possession while Salzburg relied on counterattacking, should serve as an example for the frequently discussed question: Which general match strategy or particular playing principles will most likely achieve victory? The debate tends to polarize opinion—ball possession and counterattacking. Some findings have already been compiled with the help of conventional video analysis.

Sport scientists have analysed many matches from different European leagues and looked at the connection between ball possession rate and the match result or, more specifically, goal success (Bradley et al., 2013). In contrast to previous investigations, recent studies and especially analyses collectively checking matches of the top Italian, Spanish, German, French, and English leagues argue that the connection between ball possession and match result is primarily influenced by the top teams in each league, such as FC Bayern Munich in Germany and FC Barcelona in Spain. Taking the strength of the teams into account, one can even detect a slight negative connection, implying that having less ball possession produces better results. This is corroborated by a further analysis of Champions League matches: If the best European teams play each other, ball possession rates do not tell us anything about the outcome.

In this context we are often interested in whether teams that prefer more or less ball possession show physical or technical behavior patterns depending on whether or not they are in possession. Sport scientists (Dellal et al., 2011) therefore investigated the match data for 810 players from 54 matches between teams from different positions in the English Premier League. Surprisingly, compared to the teams with less ball possession, teams with a high rate of ball possession had run,

FIGURE 18.1 Sadio Mané gets past Jérôme Boateng during a friendly match between Bayern Munich and Red Bull Salzburg (2014)

Source: Alexander Hassenstein/Bongarts/Getty Images

on average, 31 per cent further with the ball. In contrast, the average distance run without the ball, for teams with less ball possession, was around 22 per cent higher than that for teams with greater ball possession.

Teams with greater ball possession also completed more successful passes, goal-kicks, dribbling, and ball carrying into the final third of the field. In terms of ball possession, central defenders in those teams with less ball possession covered 33 per cent less distance than central defenders in teams with a greater ball possession. Interestingly, all other positions of teams with less ball possession recorded greater running distance without ball possession compared to positions of the teams were recorded in comparison to the positions of teams with greater ball possession. Wingbacks, central midfielders, and wingers with ball possession covered less distance than those in teams with a high percentage of ball possession.

Running distance covered is often connected to either ball possession or performance criteria, so players not in possession of the ball or those in a game with poorer position must run further (Figure 18.2). Or put simply: Who runs a lot wins the game.

Of course, willingness to run is essential in top league football, but it cannot be the sole factor that determines victory or defeat. Sport scientists (Lago et al., 2010) recently compared the total running distance of teams in matches of the Spanish league with match outcome and other factors (venue, quality of the opposition). In general, it appears that the overall distance covered had no influence

FIGURE 18.2 N'Golo Kanté, playing in Chelsea's midfield, tackles Philippe Coutinho of FC Liverpool (2017)

Source: Shaun Botterill/Getty Images Sport/Getty Images

on the end result. This is understandable because with a three-goal lead at half-time, the winning team does not necessarily need to expend as much physical effort in the second half.

Further results indicate that home teams cover a greater distance than visiting teams, and the better the quality of the opposition, the better the overall running performance of the other team. Surprisingly, winning teams have fewer intense physical activities (sprints of varying intensity) than losing teams and cover a greater distance running and jogging. This leads to the conclusion that players do not always exert themselves maximally, but rather utilize their energy according to the individual match.

Conversely, it is obvious that struggling teams expend greater physical effort in their attempt to better their unsatisfactory situation. These results are complemented by a statistic from the 2015–2016 Bundesliga campaign: Bayern Munich ran the least distance but won the league by a good margin.

Let's turn to the other extreme—the counterattacking game. A good example surely is RB Leipzig (Figure 18.3). Why? The tactic used by both Leipzig and Salzburg, but also by Roger Schmidt who at this time was head coach at Leverkusen, was to press the opposition very early in their own half hopefully to regain possession close to the opponent's goal area and swiftly counterattack. As everything and everybody is concentrated on winning the ball, defense is crucial. This approach was originally the radical opposite of keeping possession. Now this style is, in

FIGURE 18.3 Yussuf Poulsen and Kevin Kampl of RB Leipzig put pressure on Monaco's João Moutinho during a UEFA Champions League match (2017)

Source: Soccrates Images/Getty Images Sport/Getty Images

contrast to possession football, characterized by possession using the short ball, fewer adopted passes, but a greater overall distance covered by high-intensity runs. This strategy is best characterized by the following: "The probability of scoring a goal is higher if one does not possess the ball." Initially, although this sounds absurd for many football players, our surveys have shown that this statement is true.

Investigation by the author, using data from the 2010–2011 campaign, show that teams had significantly more goal attempts the faster they were able to win back the ball. This was especially true when the ball was won halfway up the pitch and in the opponent's defense. When relying on slow buildup play, clearly more passes are needed in order to penetrate the opposition penalty area and generate scoring chances. Furthermore, the ball can be reclaimed significantly faster the more the player sprinted when the opponent was in possession. This can be illustrated while looking at the then German Champions, Borussia Dortmund (Figures 18.4 and 18.5).

The main advantage here is that one has to cover much less space and beat fewer opposition players if the ball has already been won back in the opposition half. This model is, in contrast to popular opinion, not hard to learn. For possession football, more creativity is needed by the coach as well as by the players (Memmert, 2011, 2015). They need to act quickly, anticipate well, and have good perceptive ability.

In the future it will be possible, on the basis of positional data, to answer more precisely the question regarding the efficiency of possession and counterattacking playing styles. Our first analyses with Voronoi cells, which are presented in detail

FIGURE 18.4 İlkay Gündoğan dribbling during his first season at Borussia Dortmund (2011)

Source: Vladimir Rys/Bongarts/Getty Images

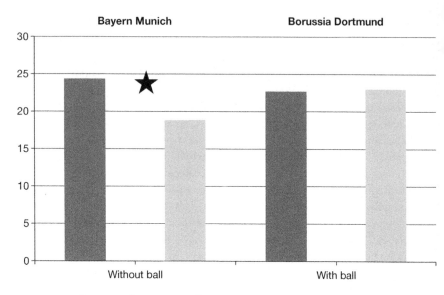

FIGURE 18.5 Dortmund's pressing index (without the ball) was significantly better than that of Bayern Munich, helping them to win the title twice

in Chapter 9, already indicate that an important parameter—spatial control—also indicates that there is going to be an exciting neck-and-neck race between these playing philosophies.

Let's first have an exemplary look at the temporal process of the counterattack. Team A develops a counterattack with player A5 on the right wing (Figure 18.7a). Waiting in the center is player A9, who also drifts out to the right wing, bringing B6 with him and thereby engaging two opponent defenders. Doing so, the team

Because of the important influence of tactical creativity on goal scoring in elite soccer (Kempe & Memmert, 2018, accepted), currently, a team at the Institute of Training and Computer Science in Sport of the German Sports University in Cologne analyses creative solutions by means of dynamic neuronal networks on the basis of positional data as input variables. The idea is that the originality of an action is expressed by the quality of a corresponding neuron: High originality is accompanied by lower frequency and a highly rated quality neuron and vice versa. In the framework of preliminarily studies (Grunz, Memmert, & Perl, 2012), the DyCoNG approach was redefined in order to simulate spontaneous creative solutions based on free associations (e.g., "jumps" between neurons, c.f. Figure 18.6). These should simplify the determination and simulation of creative action in complex matches. The basic question arises of if and how the optimized use of creative solutions can enhance the tactical performance of a team.

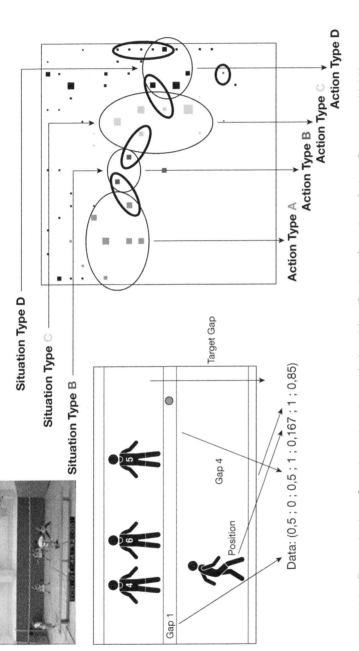

Situation Type D

Situation Type C

Situation Type B

Target Gap

Gap 4

Position

Gap 1

Data: (0,5 ; 0 ; 0,5 ; 1 ; 1 ; 0,167 ; 1 ; 0,85)

Action Type A

Action Type B

Action Type C

Action Type D

FIGURE 18.6 Determination of creative actions in match data. Identification of creative solutions from over 100,000 combinations with the help of neuronal networks. Depicted are the match situation (top left), the resulting data (bottom left), and a two-dimensional projection from a trained DyCoNG (represented by highlighted neurons), connected by clusters (thin lines), associative "jumps" between clusters (bold dotted lines), and generated quality neurons (bold lines)

controls 39.7 per cent of the space in the attacking zone in front of the opposition goal and 3.0 per cent in the penalty area. Furthermore, A9 is now able to make space for A10 and A8 at the back, the former receiving the ball from the wing (Figure 18.7b) and directly playing it to A8 (Figure 18.7c; spatial control attacking zone = 49.5 per cent; spatial control box = 18.1 per cent), who is unmarked and shoots at goal.

How does this look in terms of outplaying defenders? In Figure 18.8a one can see a well-structured attack down the wings; A4 is in ball possession, resulting in 45.1 per cent spatial control in the attacking zone and 30.8 per cent in the penalty area. With a pass through the channel (Figure 18.8b), A10 passes the ball to A11 (spatial control attacking zone = 45.3 per cent; spatial control box = 19.4 per cent). With ample space he finishes clinically. Empirically it is not yet clear whether possession or pressing and counter-pressing accomplishes more spatial control. Once coaches have come to terms with what exactly a counterattack is, computer scientists can start to program.

In the future we will be able to compare on a large scale, with Big Data, the different European leagues to each other regarding match philosophy. Currently various new sport informatics approaches are being developed to this end (Brefeld, Knauf, & Memmert, 2016). There already exist isolated studies which are generally not based on positional data, but rather from which data material is used to gain access to video footage. As an example at this point, two findings should be described (Figures 18.9 and 18.10).

Are there, for example, differences in the passing patterns between the Premier League and Primera Division? One international published study (Dellal et al., 2011) describes an analysis of 600 games in season 2006–2007, in which 5,938 passing sequences were investigated individually. The rates of successful passes and passing contact between the two teams were compared, differentiated by specific match situations (central defender, wingback, defensive midfield player etc.). In contrast to some claims, there are significantly more similarities than differences between the two leagues.

For example, the rate of successful passes varies between 70 and 81 per cent (league-independent) and no position specific difference related to the passing ratio between both leagues is indicated, but with one unexpected finding: Attackers in the Primera Division had a higher success rate with passes than those in the Premier League, who have the poorest, and also in comparison to all outfield player positions. Wingers in the Premier League have more contacts per possession than those in La Liga, while attackers in the Spanish league have more contacts per ball possession than strikers in the English Premier league.

Are there additional objective differences between the Spanish and English leagues in respect to runs and sprints? According to a study by Dellal et al. (2011), this does not really seem to be the case. Remarkably there was no difference found in the general distance covered by both teams. Also, differentiated by certain player positions (central defender, wingback, defensive midfield player, etc.), players in English teams did not run further than those of the Spanish teams.

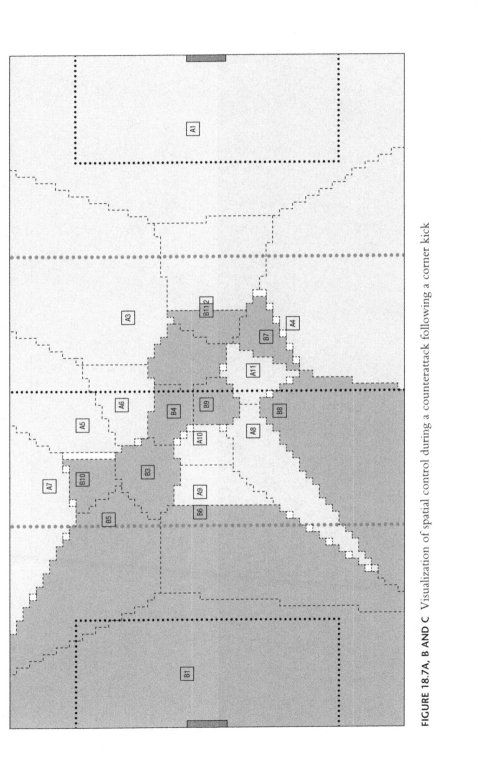

FIGURE 18.7A, B AND C Visualization of spatial control during a counterattack following a corner kick

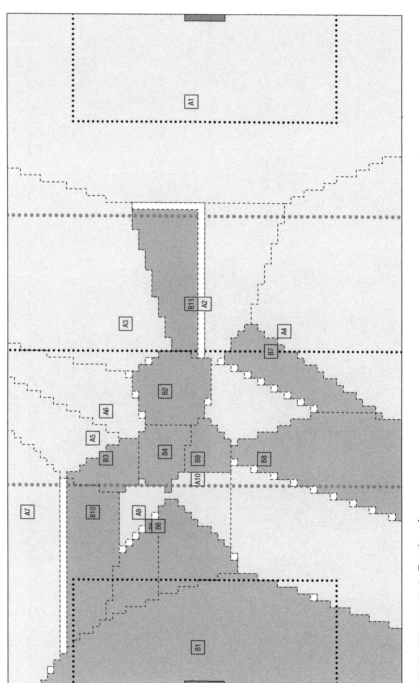

FIGURE 18.7A, B AND C Continued

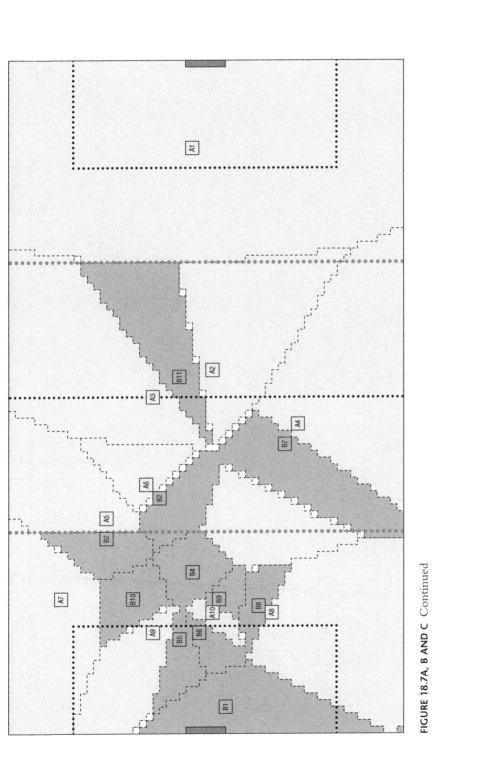

FIGURE 18.7A, B AND C Continued

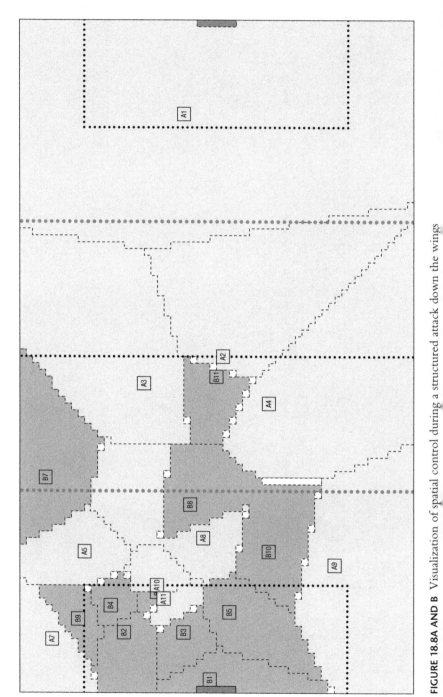

FIGURE 18.8A AND B Visualization of spatial control during a structured attack down the wings

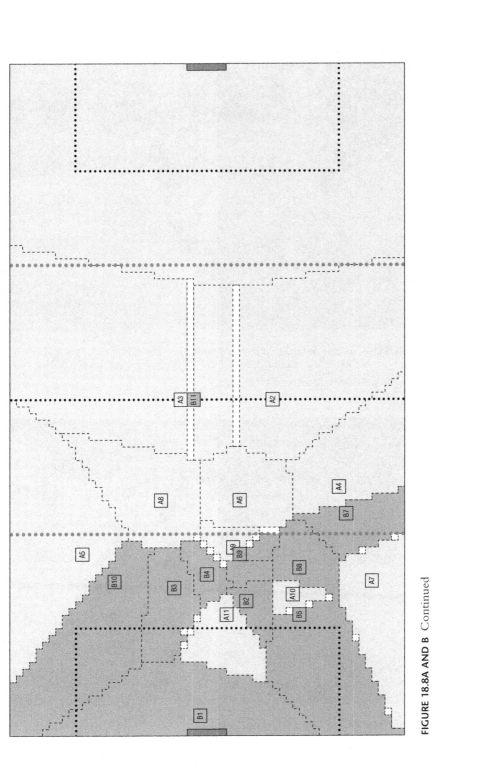

FIGURE 18.8A AND B Continued

FIGURE 18.9 Cristiano Ronaldo of Real Madrid being chased by Henrikh Mkhitaryan of Manchester United during the UEFA Super Cup final (2017)

Source: Boris Streubel—UEFA/UEFA/Getty Images

FIGURE 18.10 Álvaro Morata (Chelsea) and Koke (Atlético Madrid) run for the ball during a UEFA Champions League match (2017)

Source: Power Sport Images/Getty Images Sport/Getty Images

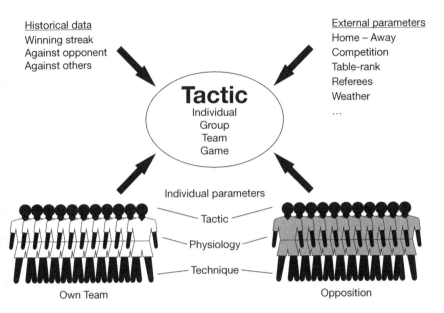

FIGURE 18.11 Factors that influence tactics in football—an overview (Rein & Memmert, 2016)

However, players in the Premier League covered a greater distance at high intensity (21–24 km/h) and very high intensity (>24 km/h) than those in the Primera Division, independent of player positions. Besides, in both leagues the defensive players ran further when not in possession and the offensive players ran further when in possession.

Therefore, the conclusion is as follows: It is not the overall distance run that plays an important role in comparison of the English and Spanish leagues—as sometimes heard in the media—but rather the quality of the distances covered, for example players' pace (Figure 18.11).

INTERVIEW WITH STEFAN WAGNER, GLOBAL GENERAL MANAGER SPORTS & ENTERTAINMENT, SAP SE

With a focus on marketing, Stefan Wagner is a graduate economist who has also completed the Sloan Executive Education program of the Massachusetts Institute of Technology. He currently works at the headquarters of SAP SE in Walldorf and is responsible for SAP's worldwide sports & entertainment branch. In his current role as a global manager for the area of sport & entertainment, Mr. Wagner puts his focus on reinforcing the distribution of sport and entertainment solutions. By intensive contact with top international customers and numerous co-innovation projects, his team supports the sustainable development of this still young branch of SAP. Close cooperation with the development teams is of central importance.

Mr. Wagner, why will the analysis of positional data revolutionize the top leagues in football?

The analysis of positional data will make this sport, which seems to become faster every day, more tactically readable and explainable. This is especially relevant for two target groups: The media—because football is a media sport and this knowledge is a fundamental component for the marketing and broadcasting of football. The management—in order to make the right decisions for the ideal match-system for the upcoming weekend matches.

In the future it will be possible, by the analysis of positional data in real time, to have a direct influence on the events during the game. This will impact in the tactics of the entire team, in attack as well as in defense, but also onto individual players. Through the use of mobile devices on the sidelines in connection with sensors, nothing will remain concealed and this enables a faster and more aimed analysis with relevant recommendations for action for the coaching staff.

How will analysis products on the basis of positional data, the likes of which we can only imagine today, look like?

The analysis of positional data in football requires new procedures and methods in order to illustrate the dynamics of the game. New machine learning-based procedures and virtual reality already set promising results. A big challenge will be to process a complicated analysis in such a way that it can be useful for the coaching staff. Analysis products therefore need to offer an intuitive and flexible user experience on the one hand, and on the other hand base on complex learning algorithms which should give an added value for match preparation and follow up reports.

INTERVIEW WITH JOHANNES HOLZMÜLLER (FIFA, HEAD OF FOOTBALL TECHNOLOGY INNOVATION)

Since 2008, Johannes Holzmüller has worked for the world football association, FIFA. He is head of the Football Technology and Innovation Department, which was established after the successful implementation of goal-line technology (GLT). In close cooperation with the IFAB (responsible for the rules of the game), his team analyzes new innovations, as for example the video assistant referee or the usage of positional data of players, and develops corresponding global standards for football. Before his time at FIFA, he worked at the sports law agency Lagardère (previously SPORTFIVE) for different football clubs in Germany.

Which role do positional data have in goal-line technology?

The GLT systems, which are currently active on the market work with positional data of the ball and a calibrated goal line. An exact determination of the ball with the help of up to seven high-speed cameras per side can therefore ensure the accuracy of the decision goal or no goal by an accuracy of 1.5 centimeters. If the ball passes the goal line, the information GOAL is shown visibly and noticeably on the referees GLT watch.

Which innovative analysis approaches can you visualize on the basis of positional data in the near future?

The goal-line technology indicated that positional data is useful for the good of the game. With the combination of visual information, tracking data and the factor time interesting innovations can be developed for various areas in football. This can be outlined by the example of the current "Video Assistant Referee" project. In this experiment the given TV pictures are combined with positional data in order to make the best camera perspectives quickly available for the video assistant referee. In general it is advisable to analyze and test in detail, because not every innovation automatically gives improvements of the game for the player and the referee and especially for the fans.

Future perspectives: towards match analysis 5.0

In this discussion it is evident that many different factors play a role in modern match analysis. This leads us directly to match analysis 5.0, in which a wide range of data from different areas will be integrated. Currently it is unclear how historical data, home and away teams, as well as external variables such as the referee, weather, and so on can be combined with tactical information at the individual, group, and team levels (Garganta, 2009; Glazier, 2015).

For example, we lack knowledge on the interaction between tactical group formations and individual technical and tactical skills (Rein, Perl, & Memmert, 2017). Of course, different positions on the field (for example, central defender, attacker) require different physical and psychological requirements, yet studies that investigate and discuss such information, in connection with tactical formations with and without the ball, are lacking (Carling et al., 2008; Rein & Memmert, 2016).

In order to implement such analyses, in Figure 18.12 a model organized by different layers is suggested (Rein & Memmert, 2016). First, the required infrastructure needs to be provided so that various information (including data on scouting, coaching, physiology, tracking, video, and psychology) can be collected. Databases must be developed in which the information can be saved securely, efficiently, and differentiated and made available.

Eventually, a process pipeline must be able to extract relevant information from the various data, in order to develop explanations and prediction models (Coutts, 2014). It should to be possible to read and visualize data on all levels. For this purpose memory capacity is needed, in order to observe the various processes and to communicate the results.

In the future, rapid analysis will be possible, selecting appropriate KPIs on the basis of positional and other data from diverse areas such as physiology, psychology, and kinesiology, and it will no longer be necessary to wait for years for the results of different European leagues to be published in scientific papers.

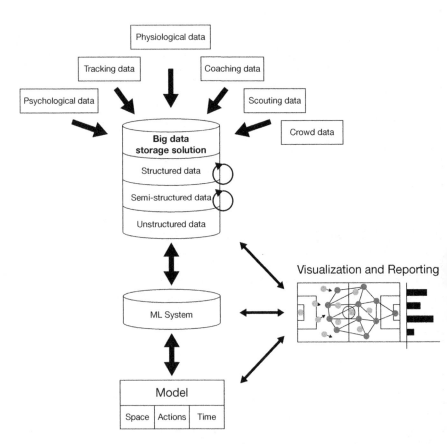

FIGURE 18.12 Big Data technology and its meaning for tactical analyses in professional football (Rein & Memmert, 2016)

In addition, more games can become included in the analysis so that reliable results will be produced. Also, by a including a greater number of players, the variation and increasing flexibility of a team can be better taken into account. This will lead to a worldwide revolution in youth and professional scouting, new match philosophies will arise, and the tactical variation will bring professional football once again to a higher level.

References

Bradley, P. S., Lago-Peñas, C., Rey, E., & Gomez Diaz, A. (2013). The effect of high and low percentage ball possession on physical and technical profiles in English FA Premier League soccer matches. *Journal of Sports Sciences, 31*, 1261–1270.

Brefeld, U., Knauf, K., & Memmert, D. (2016). Spatio-temporal convolution kernels. *Machine Learning, 102*(2), 247–273.

Carling, C., Bloomfield, J., Nelsen, L., & Reilly, T. (2008). The role of motion analysis in elite soccer: contemporary performance measurement techniques and work rate data. *Sports Med, 38*(10), 839–862.

Coutts, A. J. (2014). Evolution of football match analysis research. *Journal of Sports Science,* 32(20),1829–1830.

Dellal, A., Chamari, K., Wong, D. P., Ahmaidi, S., Keller, D., Barros, R., . . . Carling, C. (2011). Comparison of physical and technical performance in European soccer match-play: FA Premier League and La Liga. *European Journal of Sport Science, 11*, 51–59.

Garganta, J. (2009). Trends of tactical performance analysis in team sports: Bridging the gap between research, training and competition. *Revista Portuguesa de Ciências do Desporto, 9*, 81–89.

Glazier, P. S. (2015). Towards a grand unified theory of sports performance. *Human Movement Science.*

Grunz, A., Memmert, D., & Perl, J. (2012). Tactical pattern recognition in soccer games by means of special self-organizing maps. *Human Movement Science, 31*, 334–343.

Kempe, M. & Memmert, D. (2018, accepted). "Good, better, creative": The Influence of Creativity on Goal Scoring in Elite Soccer. *Journal of Sport Science.* https://doi.org/10.1080/02640414.2018.1459153

Lago, C., Casais, L., Dominguez, E., & Sampaio, J. (2010). The effects of situational variables on distance covered at various speeds in elite soccer. *European Journal of Sports Sciences, 10*, 103–109.

Memmert, D. (2011). Sports and creativity. In M. A. Runco and S. R. Pritzker (Eds.). *Encyclopedia of creativity* (pp. 373–378). San Diego, CA: Academic Press.

Memmert, D. (2015). *Teaching tactical creativity in team and racket sports: Research and practice.* Abingdon: Routledge.

Rein, R. & Memmert, D. (2016). Big data and tactical analysis in elite soccer: Future challenges and opportunities for sports science. *SpringerPlus, 5*(1), 1410.

Rein, R., Perl, R., Memmert, D. (2017). Maybe a tad early for a Grand Unified theory: Commentary on "Towards a Grand Unified Theory of sports performance" by Paul S. Glazier. *Human Movement Science, 56*, 173–175.

INDEX

Locators in *italics* refer to figures and those in **bold** to tables.

analysis program PosiCap *23*, *28*
analysis tool SOCCER 8, 31, 32, 33, 87, 122

behavior analysis 22, 32
behavior, tactical 29, 107

competition regulation 1–12
Concept Keyboards *20*
creativity 1, 11, 13, 32, 34, 122, 156, 171
creativity recognition 32

data, event 65
data, game 1, 44
data, positioning i, iii, vii, viii, ix, 1–8, 13–34, 36, 40, 41, 43, 44, 50, 53, 54, 56–59, 61, 62, 65, 67–69, 71, 72, 74, 75, 78–83, 86, 89, 91, 96, 101, 106–108, 111, 113, 118, 119, 137, 138, 156, 158, 160, 168, 169
data, tracking 2, 47, 52, 69, 169, 170

electronic performance and recording system (ELAS) 45, 46
electronic performance and tracking systems (EPTS) 45, 48, 58, 60, 61
extensively played positions 92–98

football tactics 8, 13, 16, 18, 29, 34, 48
formation/system 1–12
formation pattern approach 32

game analysis vii, 1, 2, *6*, 7, 16, 20–23, 31–33, 40, 56, 61, 86, 122
game analysis system 31
game analyst 6, *16*
game information
game observation 11, 24, 25
game philosophy 13, 160
game statistics 17, 95, 98
game systems 133–136
goal-line technology 168, 169
grid analysis (heat map) 19, 78, 79

hand notation system 16, 17, 19, 20
heat map (KPI) i, 2, 3, *6*, 7, 24, 32, 51, *79*, 87, 96, 108, 122, 147, 170
humanoid robots 29, *30*

idea (of game design) 12
interaction patterns 119

Key performance indicators (KPIs) i, ix, 2, 3, *6*, 7, 24, 26, 32, 51, 78, 87, 96, 98, 101, 108, 122, 138, 147, 170

low scaling 127–132

machine learning 8, 168, 171
match analysis i, ix, 1, 6, 8, 13, 16, 17, 19, 24–26, 29, 31, 33, 41, 45, 46, 49, 55–59, 71, 77, 79–81, 87, 98, 106, 107, 118, 138, 169, 171
match plan vii, 13

match video 22
move 13–34

neuronal clusters 40, 106, 107, 158
neuronal networks 7, 31, 32, 106, 107,
    158, *159*

optical tracking system 42

performance coefficient 24, 57, 148
performance recordings 27, 29, 57, 59, 66,
    138
physical performance 17, 27, 33, 57, 71,
    73, 74
physiological performance diagnostics 13,
    24, 25, 58, 71, 73
player position 40, 160, 167
player type 11, 108, 109
player tracking technology 20, 25, 28,
    37–39, 41, 43, 44, 46, 51, 54, 55, 61,
    71, 73, 74, 83, 169
positional data recognition 32
positional data recording 57
position recording 57
post-match game analysis 106, 118, 138
post-processing of the game 22, 40, 42
pressing 86, 101, 102, 104, 116, 117, 122,
    137–146, 158, 160
pressing index 101, 116, 122, *158*
pressing speed 102, 117
pressure efficiency 96, 142, 143, 147–149
process analysis 32, 102,109, 116
process patterns 32

radar-based tracking system 27, 44, 51
radio-based tracking system 41, 42
recognition system 20

recordings of game data 27, 29, 57, 59, 66,
    138
regeneration management 75
robot soccer 29, 33

Sabermetrics video tracking 51–54
scout 8, 9, 20, 28, 47, 53, 54, 59, 65, 66,
    69, 79, 80, 147, 170, 171
scouting 8, 9, 28, 47, 53, 54, 65, 79, 80,
    170, 171
simulative performance diagnostics 24, 25
soccer ball possession 19, 78, 82, 91, 93,
    95, 129, 153–155, 160, 171
space control values 88
space share 137–146
spatial control 87–89, *95, 104,* 124, 129,
    131, *125,* 158, 160, *161, 164*
speech pattern 20
sport informatics 25, 31, 45, 160
stress measurement 56
stress regulation 71–76
systematic game observation 24, 25

tactical orientation 124
tactical patterns ix, **7,** 32
tracking methodology 17, 24, 27, 28
tracking systems 27, 33, 41, 42, 44, 45, 48,
    51, 58, 82
tracking transponder unity 27, 37–39
training regulation 45–47
transfer game 12

virtual reality 80, 168
Voronoi cells 87, 89, 158
Voronoi diagrams 87, 88, *90,* 91

wearables 45, 54, 71–74

Made in the USA
Las Vegas, NV
14 January 2023

65617931R00103